REGENTS CRITICS SERIES

General Editor: Paul A. Olson

LITERARY CRITICISM OF
ALEXANDER POPE

Other volumes of the Regents Critics Series are:

JOSEPH CONRAD ON FICTION
Edited by Walter F. Wright

CRITICAL WRITINGS OF FORD MADOX FORD
Edited by Frank MacShane

LITERARY CRITICISM OF GEORGE HENRY LEWES
Edited by Alice R. Kaminsky

LITERARY CRITICISM OF EDGAR ALLAN POE
Edited by Robert L. Hough

Literary Criticism of
Alexander Pope

Edited by

BERTRAND A. GOLDGAR

UNIVERSITY OF NEBRASKA PRESS · LINCOLN

Copyright © 1965 by the University of Nebraska Press
All rights reserved
Library of Congress Catalog card number 64–17231

MANUFACTURED IN THE UNITED STATES OF AMERICA

Regents Critics Series

The Regents Critics Series provides reading texts of significant literary critics in the Western tradition. The series treats criticism as a useful tool: an introduction to the critic's own poetry and prose if he is a poet or novelist, an introduction to other work in his day if he is more judge than creator. Nowhere is criticism regarded as an end in itself but as what it is—a means to the understanding of the language of art as it has existed and been understood in various periods and societies.

Each volume includes a scholarly introduction which describes how the work collected came to be written, and suggests its uses. All texts are edited in the most conservative fashion consonant with the production of a good reading text; and all translated texts observe the dictum that the letter gives life and the spirit kills when a technical or rigorous passage is being put into English. Other types of passages may be more freely treated. Footnoting and other scholarly paraphernalia are restricted to the essential minimum. Such features as a bibliographical checklist or an index are carried where they are appropriate to the work in hand. If a volume is the first collection of the author's critical writing, this is noted in the bibliographical data.

PAUL A. OLSON

University of Nebraska

Contents

Contents

Introduction

THE OCCASION OF POPE'S CRITICISM

"Critics," Pope declares in an early letter to the playwright Wycherley, "as they are birds of prey, have ever a natural inclination to carrion."[1] This declaration is hardly surprising. As an aspiring poet and man of letters in Augustan England, Pope expresses a very natural scorn of the professional critic like John Dennis. His is the perennial contempt of the creative artist for his potential enemy; and that breed of man whom Swift defined as a "discoverer and collector of writers' faults" was to remain an occasional object of ridicule for Pope, as for the other satirists of his day. But despite such rather affected disparagement, Pope as a young poet was actually very much concerned with critical theory and practice. One of his earliest appearances in the literary world was with the *Essay on Criticism,* as much an art of poetry as an art of criticism, and the same letter to Wycherley which scoffs at critics also suggests a tentative solution to a vexing critical problem, the definition of wit. Throughout his career, in fact, Pope himself produced a body of literary criticism substantial enough—and perceptive enough—to place him in the first ranks of eighteenth-century critics.

His discussions of literary matters with Wycherley and other early correspondents, like the "great reading period" of his youth when he "went through all the best critics," were very much a matter of a young poet experimenting with critical ideas and creative practice, feeling his way toward an individual style and habit of mind. As Pope's reputation became more firmly established, the tentative and experimental character of his critical pronouncements disappeared; recognized achievement, it appears, gave him confidence in his own set of literary values. Nor was

1. *The Correspondence of Alexander Pope,* ed. George Sherburn (Oxford: Clarendon Press, 1956), I, 2. Cited hereafter as *Corr.*

ix

there any longer much concern with explicit literary theory. After 1712 his letters have little to offer in the way of literary criticism; and when they do, his remarks are likely to be practical advice to less successful contemporaries or critical set pieces analyzing plays or poems that have come to his attention. Similarly, his published works of criticism, except for the early *Essay*, are mostly formal examinations of specific poets or particular genres. He writes no *Spectator* papers on the psychology of the imagination (Addison), and no treatises seeking *The Grounds of Criticism in Poetry* (Dennis).

Moreover, it is significant that, again excepting the *Essay*, almost all of Pope's criticism is written as an adjunct to some other work for which he feeels responsible as either poet or editor. In other words, the principles laid down in each critical work are conditioned and modified by its immediate occasion. For this reason it is dangerous to abstract particular remarks as general statements of doctrine unless we have a sure grasp of their context, for the very questions raised in his critical prefaces and essays are determined by the nature of the creative work to which they are connected. The relationship between Pope's poetic practice and his critical justification of that practice is even more intimate than that, say, between Eliot's early poetry and early criticism.

What, then, are the questions Pope is asking in his prose criticism, and what relation do these questions bear to the immediate occasion of each work? To settle these matters of context, a brief survey of the background of each critical piece will perhaps prove helpful.

Though his first piece of criticism, the *Discourse on Pastoral Poetry*, was not published until 1717, Pope always claimed that the *Discourse* and his own *Pastorals* were both written in 1704; the most recent editor of the pastorals appears to accept his claim and suggests that Pope may have originally intended to publish the *Discourse* and the poems together.[2] At any rate, we have here a simple case of correlated theory and practice. The

2. *Pastoral Poetry and An Essay on Criticism*, ed. E. Audra and Aubrey Williams, Twickenham Edition, I (London: Methuen, 1961), pp. 13–15.

Discourse treats a genre which had recently been the subject of a minor skirmish in the great battle between Ancients and Moderns, in this instance championed respectively by the French critics Rapin and Fontenelle. In brief, Rapin, basing his ideas on the practice of Virgil and other classic pastoralists, argues that a true pastoral imitates the Golden Age in a language simple but pure. For Fontenelle, who rejects the authority of the Ancients in deference to the authority of his own reason, a pastoral merely imitates a tranquil rural life, a subject which appeals to our natural laziness. In the hands of his English followers, such as Ambrose Philips and Thomas Tickell, Fontenelle's ideas were used to justify an almost naturalistic representation of rustic language and manners.[3]

Pope's elegant *Discourse* is firmly on the side of the Ancients and Rapin, though he does make some concessions to Fontenelle. And his critical position may well be influenced by the kind of pastorals he himself wants to write. As an ambitious young poet he makes the traditional literary debut—he writes pastorals; and they are pastorals safely traditional in their imitation of classic models. The critical doctrine which accompanies them follows naturally enough: "Since the instructions for any art are to be delivered as that art is in perfection," we must derive our rules for pastorals from the practice of the Ancients. The very limited range to which Pope confines himself in these poems is given a rationale in criticism which in method is no less traditional and "neoclassical" than the poems themselves: an account, derived from classic models, of rules for the fable, manners, thoughts, and expression of a particular poetic genre or kind. Because of the uncertainties of dating their composition accurately, one hesitates to say that the *Discourse* was actually written as *post facto* justification of the *Pastorals,* though this is a distinct possibility; yet it is obvious enough that Pope's first piece of formal prose criticism, both in style and in content, is tied very closely to the manner in which he chooses to begin his career as a poet.

3. J. E. Congleton, *Theories of Pastoral Poetry in England, 1684–1798* (Gainesville: University of Florida Press, 1952), pp. 53–71.

The Preface which Pope attached to the first collected edition of his poetry in 1717 also deserves brief mention. It is likely to strike the modern reader as both beautifully polished and distressingly affected. Pope's pose is that of the humble amateur, who has written only for his own amusement, whose poems fall short of even his own ideas of poetry, and who is uncertain whether collecting his pieces is to be properly figured as "a man building a monument or burying the dead." The critical ideas of the Preface, such as they are, all stem from this affectation of humility which Pope seemed to feel the occasion demanded and which struck his friend Atterbury simply as "modesty and good sense."[4] Thus we are told that critics are too critical, that poetry and criticism are the affairs only of the idle, that poetic genius can be demonstrated only by experimentation, that since the life of a wit is a warfare upon earth, authors must be prepared to suffer, and so on. Slightly more serious is Pope's explanation of why the poems he is collecting so often imitate classic models: "Whatever is very good sense must have been common sense in all times." Nature and Homer, as the *Essay on Criticism* has told us, are the same, and "all that is left us is to recommend our productions by the imitation of the Ancients." This principle, a fairly common one in Augustan criticism, had been invoked by Addison in his review of Pope's *Essay* (*Spectator* No. 253); Pope's own enunciation of it is not as a critical dogma valuable in its own right but simply as a theoretical defense of his own poetic practice.

When we turn to Pope's criticism of Homer, we find that once again his critical ideas are oriented by the "creative" work which occasions them, in this case his translation of the *Iliad* and the *Odyssey*. The Preface to the *Iliad* (1715) has long been considered of special significance, because it has seemed that Pope was there championing the creative powers of the poetic imagination in opposition to a rigidly orthodox neoclassicism. But such a view not only does violence to the real nature of neoclassicism; as R. S. Crane points out, it is also likely to distort what Pope was actually doing in the Preface because it isolates

4. *Corr.*, I, 378.

doctrinal statements while ignoring the questions which these statements are intended to answer. And the questions which Pope raises are questions posed by the creative task he has set for himself. "His central problem," writes Professor Crane, "is dictated by the fact that he is translating the *Iliad* into modern English, and that in doing this he wishes to be as faithful as possible to the essential spirit of his great original; he must therefore decide what that essential spirit is which his rendering ought to preserve for English readers."[5] Since neither the rules for the epic nor historical study of the culture which produced it will define for us that quality which makes the *Iliad* a great poem in any age, Pope seeks his answer in the creative faculties of the poet, invention and judgment. The Preface then proceeds, by analysis and comparison, to demonstrate that the essential quality of the *Iliad* rests in the power of invention, the poetic "fire" and "rapture," in short, the imagination of its author. It is this quality which is responsible for the "beauties" of the poem's various parts and which Pope wishes to capture in his translation. To look at the Preface in this way is not to impugn the significance of its doctrine; it is simply recognizing that the doctrine is an assumption used in solving a specific problem, which arises for Pope not as critic or theorist but as poet and translator. In the same way, his notes or Observations on the *Iliad,* though they are often perceptive and interesting criticism, have as their immediate purpose Pope's effort to justify the translation of individual passages and to educate his readers to the beauties which Homer (and he) are providing.

The Postscript to the *Odyssey* (1726) also originates in Pope's desire to provide a rationale for "his" translation. The problem now, though, is not one of determining the essential spirit of the Homeric poem but rather answering a whole category of objections to its style. He must defend the *Odyssey* (and the translation bearing his name) against the charge of "lowness" and lack of sublimity, a charge made by Longinus himself. Pope begins by stating a principle of neoclassical criticism that he had

5. R. S. Crane, "On Writing the History of English Criticism, 1650–1800," *University of Toronto Quarterly*, XXII (1953), 382–383.

no need for when discussing the *Iliad*, namely that proper criticism always considers first the intention of the author and the genre of the work; it is only the execution of a subject that is liable to criticism, he says, not the nature of the subject itself. The Horatian principle of stylistic decorum is the basis for the discriminations Pope makes in answer to Longinus. The style of the *Odyssey* is that appropriate to a simple, natural narrative; it is not a lesser thing than the *Iliad*, it is only a different kind of thing. Moreover, invention and judgment are as necessary for the execution of the design of a poem like the *Odyssey* as they are for the *Iliad*. "Let it be remembered that the same genius that soared the highest, and from whom the greatest models of the sublime are derived, was also he who stooped the lowest and gave to the simple narrative its utmost perfection." Pope's method is again analytical and comparative. His comparison between the *Iliad* and the *Odyssey* is parallel to those elsewhere in his criticism between Homer and Virgil, Shakespeare and Ben Jonson, Nature and Art, except that here the comparison is designed to show not that one term is superior to the other but only that they differ. When compared to the Preface to the *Iliad*, the Postscript seems to be criticism of a sort that used to be thought of as narrowly neoclassical. That is, Pope assumes the poem to be a piece of verbal rhetoric and his critical procedure is to unfold its "beauty" by formal analysis of the rules for its poetic kind. The Preface, on the other hand, finds the sources of the *Iliad*'s "sublimity" in the creative imagination of its author. Obviously it's absurd to conclude that between 1715 and 1726 Pope suffered a relapse into a neoclassicism from which he had made a temporary recovery. The difference in approach is to be explained simply in terms of the different problems which each essay sets for itself and which must be solved if Pope's translations are to be considered successful.

In the Preface to his edition of the *Works of Shakespeare* (1725), Pope is once more writing criticism of another author intended to explain or justify labors of his own. Though he insists that he does not intend to "enter into a criticism upon this author," he immediately proceeds to do so, for his essay actually

has a double goal: to account for the nature of the text he has
had to deal with and to demonstrate both the genius and the
learning of the writer he has troubled himself to edit for his
own more polite age. Throughout Pope seems to have in mind
the objections which strict "rules-critics" (Rymer is the best
if not the only example) made to Shakespeare, especially those
involving the "irregularity" of his plays and the bombast or
vulgarity of his expression. Pope attempts to answer such objections in two ways. The first is simply to raise Shakespeare above
them in a method made traditional by Dryden, that is, by asso-
ciating him with Nature in the time-honored dichotomy of Nature
and Art. His plays, when compared to those more finished and
regular, are like "an ancient majestic piece of Gothic architecture
compared with a neat modern building: the latter is more elegant and glaring, but the former is more strong and more solemn." Pope's second technique for answering the charges against
his dramatist is more interesting and represented less a cliché
in the early eighteenth century than the first. He uses a principle
of historical criticism to explain that the defects of Shakespeare's
plays come from the nature of the age in which they were written,
an age when critical learning was in short supply and when play-
wrights were forced to pander to the debased taste of their
audience. "To judge therefore of Shakespeare by Aristotle's
rules is like trying a man by the laws of one country who acted
under those of another." The same critical principle is used in
the last part of the Preface to explain defects of expression and
corruptions of the text, both of which are laid at the door of
the ignorant players who were Shakespeare's early editors. It is
in this manner, then, that Pope uses his Preface both to explain
the difficulties he has encountered when performing "the dull
duty of an editor" and to defend and exhibit the artistic excellence of the dramatist he has seen fit to edit. This latter part of
his task, which he calls the better half of criticism, he completes
in the text of the plays themselves by marking "shining passages" in the margin.

One final group of Pope's writings remains to be considered
in this survey of the occasions of his critical works—namely, criti-

cism written in the form of satire. In the harsh and sometimes despairing assessment of eighteenth-century culture made by Pope and such friends as Swift, Gay, and Arbuthnot, literary offenses naturally ranked high among the butts of ridicule. Pope's own attacks on literary figures or practices often have personal quarrels as their immediate context; they emerge from particular episodes in his life as a wit, his "warfare upon earth." But beneath the personal motive of such satire, as beneath that of all the Tory wits, is that more impersonal voice of the satirist decrying the collapse of humanistic ideals, the barbarization of taste, the end of a civilizing tradition: "Art after Art goes out, and all is Night." As a part of their general indictment of the shifting values of his age, many of Pope's satiric poems, especially the *Dunciad* and the *Epistle to Augustus,* include much that could properly be called literary criticism. In making selections for this volume, though, I have thought it advisable to restrict the satiric pieces to two works in prose which are directed completely at literary objects, *Guardian* No. 40 and *Peri Bathous, or The Art of Sinking in Poetry.* They differ from Pope's other criticism only in their satiric form; critical principles are implicit in each.

As a matter of fact, *Guardian* No. 40 (April 27, 1713) has its origin in a dispute involving literary theory as well as personal animus. Five previous essays in Steele's *Guardian* were devoted to a discussion of pastoral poetry; the critic, presumably Thomas Tickell, expounded the rationalistic arguments of Fontenelle to the disparagement of the neoclassic pastorals and defended the use of details drawn from English rustic life. The last of the five papers, in particular, lauded the modern pastoralist Ambrose Philips as the rightful heir of Theocritus, Virgil, and Spenser. Pope, whose own pastorals had appeared in the same volume of Tonson's *Miscellanies* as Philips's, was mentioned only once, and even then it was in a manner hardly calculated to appease wounded pride. For in *Guardian* No. 30 Tickell praised Pope for his entertaining use of elves and fairies in poetry; but the passage he quotes as example is not from Pope's pastorals but from his rendering of Chaucer's *Merchants Tale.* Thus, in a stroke worthy of Pope himself, Tickell simultaneously suggests that

Pope is praiseworthy only when translating Chaucer and aligns
him with the tendency of the "modern" school to replace classic
myth with English folklore, a tendency Pope disapproved of.[6] It
was to answer this double affront to his person and his principles
that Pope wrote his own *Guardian* paper.

In the essay, Pope of course pretends to be the same critic
who has written the other papers on the pastoral and who is now
making amends for his failure to discuss Mr. Pope. His irony
is obvious enough ("Mr. Pope hath fallen into the same error
with Virgil"), and once allowance is made for the satiric form
of the essay, his ideas about pastoral turn out to be pretty much
the same as those in his *Discourse*. Less obvious, perhaps, is the
fact that his irony here turns on the manipulation of critical
terms he defines elsewhere. In the *Discourse* Pope makes a distinction between simplicity and rusticity; the Preface to the *Iliad*
elaborates the point: "There is a graceful and dignified simplicity,
as well as a bald and sordid one, which differ as much from each
other as the air of a plain man from that of a sloven. . . . Simplicity is the mean between ostentation and rusticity." But in
Guardian No. 40 that distinction is deliberately discarded. The
major premise for his ironic praise of Philips is that "simplicity"
means banal "rusticity"; once the equation of the two terms has
been established, Pope can even praise Philips for his "propriety,"
his adherence to the style demanded by the genre. In the same
way, "imitation," always an honorific word, is here taken to
mean only direct copying, so that Pope can seem to speak in a
traditional manner of Philips's poems while actually ridiculing
him for stealing wholesale. It is in this very indirect manner that
Pope's satiric revenge incorporates serious criticism.

Though it was not published until March 7, 1727/28, *Peri
Bathous* actually originated in the years of the famous Scriblerus
Club (1713–1714), that group of Tory wits (Swift, Pope, Parnell,
Gay, Arbuthnot, and the Earl of Oxford) who undertook a com-
plicated scheme for satirizing the follies of all fields of learning
through the mask of a fictitious pedant, Martinus Scriblerus.

6. Daniel A. Fineman, "The Motivation of Pope's *Guardian* 40," *MLN*,
LXVII (1952), 24–28.

Since the piece originated as a Scriblerian project, there has been some questioning of Pope's authorship, especially since it is known that Arbuthnot had a hand in it as well. However, there seems to be little question that Pope was primarily responsible for the treatise as it was finally published, and scholars have in general been willing to accept his account of the matter to Swift, "I have entirely methodized and in a manner written it all."[7] He goes on to promise Swift, "It will be a very instructive piece."

And instructive it is. Like the *Dunciad*, published a short time later and directed at much the same group of mediocre writers, its background involves all the complexities of Pope's personal quarrels with the Dunces; but, again like the *Dunciad*, it rises above the ridicule of individuals to make a serious assessment of contemporary letters and contemporary morality. It is an *Ars Poetica* in ironic dress, as Pope himself indicated when he remarked to Spence, "*The Profound*, though written in so ludicrous a way, may be very well worth reading seriously as an art of rhetoric."[8] And how are we to read *Peri Bathous* in this way? By a simple process of reversing the ironic statements so that we equate poetic virtues with everything Martinus condemns and poetic vices with all that he recommends. Such a reading may seem too mechanical to be true, but Pope's irony in this prose work has few of the subtle involutions we look for in Swift, and the satiric framework provided by the persona is maintained with considerable consistency. About the only places where the irony is broken are Martinus' comments on particular passages, where he points out inconsistencies in a manner not unlike that of straightforward criticism. Of course, this is not to suggest that the satire of *Peri Bathous* is not complex, for ironic reversal of value statements is only one of Pope's devices. Almost as important here is the Swiftian technique of verbal literalism: Martinus

7. *Corr., II*, 468; on the Scriblerus club see *The Memoirs...of Martinus Scriblerus*, ed. Charles Kerby Miller (New Haven: Yale University Press, 1950); on the background of *Peri Bathous*, see the edition by Edna Leake Steeves (New York: King's Crown Press, 1952).

8. Joseph Spence, *Anecdotes, Observations, and Characters of Books and Men*, ed. S. W. Singer (London, 1820), p. 176.

takes "low" in a purely physical sense, he translates Horace's "prodesse" as "to profit" financially, he relates "mediocre" to the Golden Mean, and so on. This method enables Pope both to degrade bad art and artists by physically low associations and to provide Martinus with a specious logic ridiculous in itself.

But it is *Peri Bathous* as a critical document that concerns us here. If we take Pope's hint and read it "seriously," we find that its underlying ideas are no different from those in his other criticism—in short, all the familiar, urbane dicta of the classical tradition. These ideas will be surveyed in the second part of this introduction, but it may be well at this point to indicate a few of the principles indirectly expounded in *Peri Bathous*. Pope's treatise is modeled on Longinus' *Peri Hupsous (On the Sublime)*, which remains in the background as a critical norm. Although the eighteenth-century movement of aesthetic speculation about the sublime was a later development, and one in which Pope had little share, Longinus' reputation was high in his day;[9] and *Peri Hupsous* could easily be used as the implicit standard of value in *Peri Bathous,* just as a true epic functions normatively in a mock-epic. Thus Pope associates the "sublime," the "heights of Parnassus," with the Ancients and the "bathetic" with the Moderns. Throughout the treatise, in fact, the practice of the Ancients is the center of value. It is partly for this reason that the ludicrous examples are all drawn from contemporary writers, especially that author of wretched epics and perennial butt of the wits, Sir Richard Blackmore. But even in this attack directed completely at the Moderns, Pope's attitude toward the Ancients is not mere slavish veneration of authority, for we are enjoined (by implication) to imitate their virtues, not their imperfections, and we are cautioned that "rules" are insufficient without genius. Moreover, "common sense" is essential to the artist if his work is to have uniformity of design and imitate nature; "nature" here means "actuality," and its imitation produces verisimilitude or adherence to probability. "Peculiarity" of thinking produces "unaccountable" images. Common sense also dictates observance

9. S. H. Monk, *The Sublime* (Ann Arbor: Ann Arbor Paperbacks, University of Michigan Press, 1960), pp. 22–23.

of decorum; discordant "kinds" and inappropriate diction are among the chief sins. Since *Peri Bathous* is an inverted rhetorical treatise, Pope attacks a whole host of errors in expression: prolixity, farfetched or over-extended or mixed metaphors, anti-climax, technical jargon, and so on. Throughout this part of the discourse, the criteria are those which Pope emphasizes every-where—clarity and consistency and good sense. It is excess, the "abuse of speech," that is the enemy.

Though such a resumé hardly does justice to *Peri Bathous,* perhaps it will suggest how Pope's burlesque treatise can be used as a source of critical principles, despite the fact that neither its origin nor its form are those of ordinary formal criticism. For that matter, as the foregoing survey has indicated, none of Pope's prose criticism has as its primary goal the presentation of literary theory per se. Each piece is occasioned by events in his career as a creative artist or a besieged wit, events external to a purely critical purpose. Consequently, the extraction of critical doc-trine from his prefaces and essays is risky if we fail to relate that doctrine to the genetic and contextual background which prompts Pope to ask the questions that he does. To say this, of course, is not to minimize the value of the criticism itself, nor is it to suggest that his theoretical ideas are so flexible as to be non-existent. The argument of each of his critical works, though shaped and modified by its immediate occasion, also is controlled by assumptions about the nature, purpose, or method of imagina-tive literature. What these assumptions are we may now proceed to inquire.

CRITICAL PRINCIPLES

Since Pope's criticism must be viewed against the background of English neoclassicism perhaps a few cautionary remarks about that troublesome term will be useful before we try to formulate his own critical principles. When we call him a neoclassical critic we are, first of all, placing him in a tradition of literary criticism based not only on the writings of Aristotle and Horace but also on their Renaissance and seventeenth-century interpre-ters. The *Essay on Criticism* is testimony to Pope's wide reading

in the classical critics; its precepts are synthesized from an enor-
mous variety of sources: Aristotle, Horace, Quintilian, Longinus, Vida, the French critics Rapin, Le Bossu, Bouhours, Boileau,
Restoration critics like Dryden, Walsh, Roscommon, and so on.
And Pope's early reading of "all the best critics" is reflected not
only in the *Essay* but in all his criticism. In the second place,
one distinguishing mark of this tradition, though by no means
the only one or always present, is the tendency to regard a poem
as a species of the art of rhetoric, designed both to have an
effect on its reader and to exist independently as a piece of craftsmanship. As a corollary to this rhetorical approach the different
genres were ranked in a poetic hierarchy, with each genre or
"kind" having its own rules of craft. Pope, for example, ven-
erates the epic as the highest of the kinds, and approaches the
subject of pastorals or the *Iliad* or Voltaire's *Henriade* with the
assumption that each particular kind is to be analyzed according
to rules derived from classic practice—rules for fable, manners,
expression, and so forth.

It is partly the existence of such rules that has produced a
good bit of misunderstanding about neoclassicism. It used to
be fashionable to cite the rules as evidence of the extraordinary
rigidity and authoritarianism of neoclassical criticism. But all
students of the eighteenth century now recognize that such a
characterization of the movement is inaccurate, to say the least.
Neoclassicism, at least in England, was neither so inflexible nor
so simple a tradition. There were rules, certainly, but no critic
of any significance regarded them as unbreakable laws, or, indeed,
as anything other than an attempt to make the successful practice of the Ancients easily available to modern writers. When
Addison declared, "There is sometimes a greater judgment
shown in deviating from the Rules of Art than in adhering to
them" (*Spectator* No. 592), or when Pope portrayed himself as
"saucy enough to think that one may sometimes differ from
Aristotle without blundering" and as "sure one may sometimes
fall into an error by following him servilely" (*Postscript*), they
were not being rebellious or perverse. They were saying what
Dryden, Temple, Dennis, Congreve, Farquhar had also said; to

voice reservations about strict applicability of the rules was, in
Pope's day, a little like declaring oneself against sin. Nor is the
charge of authoritarianism any more cogent. One of the themes
of the *Essay on Criticism,* of course, is that the rules are "nature
still, but nature methodized," and again the precept is a com-
monplace. Critics seldom failed to point out that the rules were
based on reason and nature, not simply on authority.

Perhaps a comment on one other misconception about neoclassicism, though it is seldom encountered any more, may be
helpful to that reader of Pope's criticism who has fed mostly
on a romantic diet. This is the old notion that the neoclassical
tradition, with its emphasis on the proper rules for art, neglected
the role of original genius, of imagination, or even of feeling in
the creation of a literary work. This, too, misrepresents what
critics of the period were actually saying. There were certainly
plenty of warnings in the period against unbridled imagination
or "enthusiasm" in intellectual prose, such as treatises on religion or ethics. But poetry was another matter altogether. However much the critics may have cautioned against the excess and
extravagance wrought by an uncontrolled fancy, they never
denied that imagination or invention is essential to the creation
of art as well as judgment.[10] What was admired was a proper
balance or harmony of the creative and controlling faculties, not
the cold correctness of a literature produced only by reason and
the rules. In the *Essay on Criticism* Pope insists that precepts are
sometimes inadequate, that the greatest beauties spring from
a "grace beyond the reach of art"; and behind his words is a
whole critical tradition which recognizes the irregular, the spontaneous, the irrational elements in art.[11] As we have seen, Pope
praises Homer mainly for the "fire" of his imagination, Shakespeare for the naturalness of his genius. He insists in several
places that the most material part of a tragedy is "moving the
passions," and remarks of Otway, " 'Tis a talent of nature, rather

10. D. F. Bond, "Distrust of Imagination in English Neo-Classicism,"
Philological Quarterly, XIV (1935), 54–69.
11. See S. H. Monk, " 'A Grace Beyond the Reach of Art,' " *Journal of the
History of Ideas,* V (1944), 131–150.

than an effect of judgment, to write so movingly."[12] If we label such statements pre-romantic, it can only be that our approach to Pope's day is a teleological chase, with Wordsworth and Coleridge as the beasts in view. Nor will the term "liberal" do much better, for any neoclassical orthodoxy so rigid as to make Pope's ideas seem radical is an orthodoxy invented by the historians, not practiced by the Augustans.

In fact, to come to Pope's criticism with any doctrinal preconceptions about liberal or orthodox, neoclassic or romantic, is likely to be misleading. Much saner is the approach suggested by R. S. Crane, who points out that the neoclassical commonplaces existed not as a unified doctrine but as a critical vocabulary flexible enough to accommodate many varying critical systems. And the flexibility of this critical language derived from its characteristic manipulation of contraries.[13] "A play ought to be a *just* and *lively* image of human nature ... for the *delight* and *instruction* of mankind." So Dryden defines dramatic art. In the same way, Pope's prose criticism is frequently organized around such antithetic terms as these: invention and judgment, nature and art, the irregular and the regular, fancy and learning, originality and imitation, the genius and the artist, the charming and the correct, the sublime and the beautiful, the pleasing and the instructive, the exotic and the probable. Moreover, the couplets of the *Essay on Criticism* consistently point up similar antitheses, for it is a part of the design of that poem to reconcile the apparent dichotomies of nature and the rules, wit and judgment, and so on. Though it is safe to say that by and large Pope tends to emphasize the terms which relate to literature as an art and consequently to stress judgment, this is by no means always the case. So much depends on the context of the critical statement, on whether he is evaluating a genius of the past or giving rules for writing pastorals in the present. But to say—and it has been said—that Pope gradually emancipates himself from the rigid neoclassicism of the *Essay* and adopts a more liberal

---

12. Spence, *Anecdotes, Observations, and Characters*, p. 215.
13. Crane, "On Writing the History of English Criticism," pp. 384–385.

position is to ignore both the nature of his criticism and the wide range of the neoclassical critical vocabulary.

The critical tradition which Pope worked in was thus neither an authoritarian, nor a coldly rational, nor an inflexible approach to literature. The judiciousness and balance of Pope's own critical statements are characteristic of the entire movement. But though he shared with his contemporaries that fundamental attitude toward art which we call neoclassical, there was still plenty of room for individual expression. Within the broad tradition there were ideas, terms, or assumptions that had special significance for Pope.

We may examine first some words and concepts which relate either to the nature of literary art in general or to the process by which it is created. Like any other neoclassicist, Pope accepts the Aristotelian doctrine that art is an imitation of Nature. The problem, though, is just what Pope means by "nature." In the *Essay on Criticism,* there are these famous lines, addressed ostensibly to critics but meant for poets as well:

> Unerring Nature, still divinely bright,
> One clear, unchanged, and universal light,
> Life, force, and beauty, must to all impart,
> At once the source, and end, and test of Art.

We may well grumble along with John Dennis, the *Essay's* first critic, that these lines are irritatingly vague. But Pope was using a familiar conception, one which goes back to the Stoics and to Plato: Nature as universal and permanent order. As an object of imitation it meant, in A. O. Lovejoy's words, "the universal and immutable in thought, feeling, and taste; what has always been known, what everyone can immediately understand and enjoy."[14] Since the writings of the Ancients embody this universal principle and since the rules are only rational ways of describing their success, there is no disharmony between nature, classical authority, and the rationalistic canons of art. Elsewhere, however, even in the same poem, Pope uses Nature to mean "natural-

---

14. " 'Nature' as Aesthetic Norm," *Essays in the History of Ideas* (New York: George Braziller, 1955), p. 73.

ness," or freedom from rules, tradition, or convention; in this sense Nature is the antithesis of Art and refers more to the creative source than to the object to be imitated. Thus Pope praises Shakespeare as "not so much an imitator as an instrument of Nature." Finally, in still other places, Pope sometimes equates Nature with actuality, things as they really are. "False eloquence," for example, is objectionable because it hides "the face of Nature."

Those are some of the primary meanings of "nature" in Pope's usage, though the listing is far from complete. But how is she to be imitated? What criteria are derived from the premise that Nature is to be followed? The most obvious is universality; the artist portrays the general, not the individual, and attends to the representation of *la belle nature,* the ideal, not to particularities or little exactnesses. Since Pope had, in the *Essay,* given Nature the traditional meaning of a universal norm, he would accept this principle of imitation which follows from it. But elsewhere he sounds quite willing to praise that poet who numbers the streaks of the tulip. In a note to Book VI of the *Iliad,* he praises Homer for his use of small details and concludes: "This alone might be a confutation of that false criticism some have fallen into, who affirm that a poet ought only to collect the great and noble particulars in his painting." He is careful, of course, in another note, to condemn naturalistic representation of "trivial particulars," such as can be supplied by a reader's imagination.

The fact is that in Pope's practical criticism "Nature" usually means actuality, empirical reality, and the criterion of imitation is verisimilitude.[15] "Every single character in Shakespeare is as much an individual as those in life itself," Pope writes; and the chief beauty of Homer's characterizations is that he has not hesitated to mix virtues and vices realistically: "We should know that the poet has rather studied Nature than perfection in the laying down his characters." In *Peri Bathous,* as already noted, Martinus recommends the anti-natural way of thinking to the would-be master of the Bathos: "His eyes should be like unto the wrong end of a perspective glass, by which all the objects of

15. Sense 1 in Lovejoy's analysis, *Ibid.,* p. 70.

Nature are lessened." It need hardly be said that Pope is no naturalist. But his interpretation of verisimilitude and probability made allowance for the individual as well as the typical, and he consistently attacked that writer who failed to keep his eye on the object.

In placing some stress on the rendition of particular, visible nature as well as on the ideal or the general, Pope was doing nothing that would strike his contemporaries as new or odd. They would associate it with the traditional rhetorical criterion of *enargeia*—pictorial vividness, or, in Pope's words, "the liveliness of painting." The notion of vividness is indeed part of the larger neoclassical doctrine which urges a parallel between the sister arts, poetry and painting.[16] A casual phrase of Horace, *ut pictura poesis*, was gradually elevated into full-blown dogma, and the assumption that poems should be like paintings is a major motif in the criticism of Pope, himself a painter, especially in his remarks on Homer. Between Books XVIII and XIX of the *Iliad* Pope provides an entire essay analyzing Homer's description of the shield as a "complete idea of painting and a sketch for what one may call an universal picture." And in note after note on the *Iliad* we are made to understand that because Homer is successful pictorially, he is successful poetically.

Whatever the manner of artistic imitation, its purpose, for Pope as for all neoclassicists, is expressed in the twofold Horatian formula, to instruct and to delight. That Pope adhered to the doctrine that poetry must be instructive as well as pleasing needs little comment; everyone is familiar with his defense of his satires as moral art. In his criticism the didactic function of art receives little explicit comment, but it is always taken for granted. There is little reason to doubt his sincerity when he asserts that the chief aim of the *Iliad* is to instruct and that he who misses the morality of that poem is reading it as "common romance." This is not merely a conventional remark made out of deference to Madame Dacier, Le Bossu, or other traditional critics of Homer. Pope's whole corpus of critical remarks on the poem is governed

16. Jean Hagstrum, *The Sister Arts* (Chicago: University of Chicago Press, 1958), pp. 135–136.

by what he considers Homer's controlling design, a design in which the pleasing and the instructive are inseparable.[17] Homer does not wander in fancy's maze, Pope is saying; the action of the poem constitutes a moral drama of significance to any age. And it is hardly surprising that very prominent among the shining passages which Pope marks in his edition of Shakespeare are those which express sententiously some universal truth.[18] Though he would interpret "moral" in a fairly broad way, Pope doubtless gave hearty assent to the opinion sent him by Atterbury, "that poetry without a moral is a body without a soul."[19]

Poetry, then, is an imitation of Nature toward the end of instructing and delighting. But what are the sources of this imitation? The two primary terms in Pope's criticism have been discussed already: invention and judgment. For Pope (to recapitulate) invention means the boldness of the creative imagination; it is associated with "Nature" and with "genius" and is sometimes characterized in metaphors of fire or of growth ("vigorous seed," "wild paradise"). Judgment is the controlling faculty, associated with regularity, order, method, probability, design, and "Art." The two terms are held in balance by Pope, with the emphasis shifting according to the context and occasion of the critical piece. Nowhere, though, does he *exclude* one faculty in favor of the other; the notes to Homer laud his judgment almost as much as the Preface does his invention. One other term relating to the creative process, one less easy to deal with, is "wit." It appears to have had considerable significance for Pope in his early correspondence and in the *Essay on Criticism*. There is no need to describe here the way its multiplicity of meanings operate poetically in the *Essay*,[20] but it is necessary to indicate briefly some of its primary senses. One meaning of wit

17. See Douglas Knight, *Pope and the Heroic Tradition* (New Haven: Yale University Press, 1951), pp. 19–20.
18. See John Butt, *Pope's Taste in Shakespeare* (London: Oxford University Press, 1936), *passim*.
19. *Corr.*, I, 502.
20. See William Empson, *The Structure of Complex Words* (London: Chatto and Windus, 1951), pp. 84–100.

is the dazzling expression, the startling conceit, verbal brilliance; it is wit in this sense, the wit of the metaphysicals, that Pope attacks in his letters to Wycherley. Method and harmony, he insists, are essential to "true wit." In the *Essay* Pope goes much farther. Wit is there associated with invention, with the source of all art, and it is sometimes clearly distinguished from judgment—and sometimes not. In the view of recent scholars, Pope is participating in a contemporary controversy which involves the defence of wit (i.e., all imaginative literature) in an increasingly scientific age. A sharp distinction between wit and judgment would support the increasingly popular attitude that literary expression is only ornament, that real insight can be provided only by judgment, preferably expressing itself in cold, hard prose. Instead, to validate literature, Pope elevates wit into a faculty which, as La Rochefoucauld put it, "pierces into the very bottom of things." It is a mode of insight special to literary art; and it is inseparable (at least in several couplets of the poem) from judgment, the methodizing faculty, and from Nature, the immutable and universal order.[21]

So far we have looked at the general neoclassical assumptions which informed Pope's criticism, assumptions about the kind of Nature which art is to imitate, and about the manner, the goal, and the sources of that imitation. But there are other principles about more particular matters which are equally important for Pope when he engages in the immediate critical job of analyzing one work or one genre. The first of these, of course, is the doctrine of the "kinds"; as he makes clear in the Postscript to the *Odyssey*, practical criticism must begin by determining the genre, the traditional kind of poem which the author intended to write. Once this is done, the critic may examine how well it lives up to what readers expect of poems of its type. As we shall see, the notion that a poet writes in a traditional kind is the basis for the principle of decorum in style.

21. E. N. Hooker, "Pope on Wit: The *Essay on Criticism*," in *The Seventeenth Century: Studies in the History of English Thought and Literature by R. F. Jones and Others* (Stanford: Stanford University Press, 1951), pp. 225–246. See also Audra and Williams, *Pastoral Poetry*, pp. 213–219.

When the poem is approached from the perspective of its kind, there are criteria by which we may judge its execution; for Pope they fell into three groups, which he called the three *tours* in poetry: the design, the language, and the versification.[22] Each of these categories figures large in his applied criticism, but design is in general the most significant of the three. As critics we are instructed to "survey the whole, nor seek slight faults to find," and as writers we are expected to realize

> 'Tis not a lip, or eye, we beauty call
> But the joint force and full result of all.

For Pope, "design" means a totality of structure, an organic unity which subsumes the individual parts and to which each incident, each image, every detail must contribute. Even Horace's *Ars Poetica* itself is deprecated for lacking "the regularity that flows from the following a plan."[23] And the same criterion is employed frequently in the notes to the *Iliad*, where Pope finds the whole design to be governed by the moral, the wrath of Achilles. With this principle of unity as his thesis, he argues that the last two books are not "excrescencies, but essential to the poem," and defends the "machinery" of messages to the gods as "necessary, and consequently a beauty to the poem."

The language which expresses the design must conform to the ancient principle of decorum, "for different styles with different subjects sort." This rule, that the style must be appropriate to the kind, is the basis for the discriminations Pope makes in defending the *Odyssey* against the strictures of Longinus and for the distinction between the "simple" and the "rustic" in his writings on pastorals. When correcting the language of a poem, Pope told Spence, one should ask oneself questions about stylistic decorum: "If an elegy, 'these lines are very good, but are not they of too heroical a strain?' and so *vice versa*."[24] Occasionally, Pope is forced to defend the presence of low images in the *Iliad*, but he always does so with some embarrassment. For the

22. Spence, *Anecdotes, Observations, and Characters*, p. 23.
23. *Ibid.*, p. 1.
24. *Ibid.*, p. 24.

most part, he finds decorum in style one of his most useful critical tools. But language must not only suit the occasion; it must be correct. Affected diction, false wit, technical jargon, antiquated expressions, new coinages, and the like are attacked both in the *Essay on Criticism* and in *Peri Bathous.* They not only are offences against propriety but come between the reader and his perception of the "face of Nature." Early in his career, Pope was advised by the poet Walsh to make correctness his study and aim, since this was the "one way left of excelling."[25] Though correctness covers a wider ground than language, Pope obviously felt correct diction to be a *sine qua non* of following nature; and he did not hesitate to judge others by what he had presumably taken as an ideal for himself.

About the third of the three *tours,* versification, Pope had a great deal to say, most of it self-explanatory. His own rules of prosody, set forth in one of his letters, testify to his perennial concern with craftsmanship, even though he does not always follow these rules himself.[26] One which he *does* follow, and which recurs with some frequency throughout his criticism, is that "the sound must seem an echo to the sense." This principle of imitative or representative meter, attacked by Dr. Johnson and defended by many modern theorists, has also been seen as one more effort to preserve the literary way against the attack of empirical science; sound is not mere ornament but is to be integrated with meaning in a way that will bring poetic imitation into harmony with the nature revealed by scientific observation.[27] But whatever its rationale, the doctrine was clearly of special importance to Pope, who boasted to Spence, "I have followed the significance of the numbers, and the adapting them to the sense, much more even than Dryden, and much oftener than any one minds it."[28]

25. *Ibid.,* p. 280.
26. See Jacob H. Adler, "Pope and the Rules of Prosody," *PMLA,* LXXVI (1961), 218–226.
27. Dean Tolle Mace, "The Doctrine of Sound and Sense in Augustan Poetic Theory," *Review of English Studies,* (n.s.) II (1951), 129–139.
28. Spence, *Anecdotes, Observations, and Characters,* p. 316.

These, then, are some of Pope's criteria for formal excellence. One final strain of thought in his criticism is of another order altogether, and, in fact, seems almost to run counter to neoclassical formalism. I refer to what we now think of as historical criticism, the attempt to illuminate works of the past by reference to the ethos, audience, or literary practice of the age when they were written. In Pope's hands the historical approach, which became quite popular before the century ended, is used not so much to explain as to explain *away* the faults of those writers of the past whose genius raised them above correctness and the rules. The obvious example is the Preface to *Shakespeare*, whose defects are blamed on the Elizabethan theater and the acting profession in general. It is a point, incidentally, which Pope evidently took very seriously, for he once explained that he himself never wrote for the stage because he realized "how much everybody that did . . . was obliged to subject themselves to the players and the town."[29] In his Homer, too, we find Pope extenuating through historical argument certain parts of the poem which might strike his readers as offensive. He warns, for example, against our being shocked at the number of images drawn from rural life, explaining that in ancient times agriculture was the occupation of the highest, not the lowest people. But Pope cannot maintain the historical approach with any consistency; he is, after all, translating Homer for his own refined age, and he seems uneasily aware of the difficulties that arise when the taste of that age—his own taste—is brought up against a relative standard of value. So it is that after justifying a low image in Homer he is forced to conclude, "However, upon the whole, a translator owes so much to the taste of the age in which he lives, as not to make too great a compliment to the former; and this induced me to omit the mention of the word *ass* in the translation."

CRITIC AND POET

Pope's method as a critic is singularly levelheaded. It has been remarked often enough that he is influenced by Longinus and

29. *Ibid.*, p. 197.

the School of Taste, that he ridicules slavish rules-critics. It ought also to be noted that the obverse is true, that he has only contempt for those who extol the "simplicity," the *"je ne sais quoi,"* the "genius" of the Ancients, without giving us reasons. Some critics, says Pope, "are always giving us exclamations instead of criticisms." Pointing out beauties is the "better half" of criticism, but this does not mean wondering with a foolish face of praise. Critical procedure is to be governed, in his estimation, by logic, order, and reason. At the same time, though, it would be a mistake to expect Pope's rational method to produce a coherent system. He is not systematic because he is an occasional and not a professional critic. However, what appears to be a lack of system is really only a lack of explicitness; for his judgments are all framed in traditional critical language and all formed by a traditional way of looking at life and art. Taken as a whole, Pope's literary criticism is marked by the judiciousness, the eclecticism, the flexibility, the attempt to harmonize opposing attitudes characteristic of the best minds of the neoclassical tradition.

It is a tradition, a habit of mind, which the reader of Pope's poetry needs to recapture. It may be true, as W. K. Wimsatt has argued, that Augustan rhetorical theory had outrun Augustan poetic practice. His point is that the decline of rhetoric in the face of scientific assault gave rise to a theoretical emphasis upon the plain style, whereas in actual practice Pope's verse is only superficially plain statement: it has its own way of "framing and forcing implicit metaphoric alignments and ironic confrontations."[30] Yet this argument, important as it is, has to do mainly with the rhetorical figures, and neoclassical criticism had other wares to offer. A glance at the bibliography appended to this introduction will reveal some of the uses to which Pope's criticism has already been put in a reading of his poetry. His ideal of correctness—in imitation of nature, in design, language, and versification—has helped to demonstrate some of the subtleties of his craftsmanship (Tillotson); his remarks on Homer have

30. W. K. Wimsatt, Jr., and Cleanth Brooks, *Literary Criticism: A Short History* (New York: Knopf, 1957), p. 233.

provided insight into his translation of the *Iliad* (Knight); and the doctrine of the "kinds," of the different levels of style recognized in Pope's day, has furnished the basis for an illuminating approach to the *Rape of the Lock,* the *Imitations of Horace,* the *Moral Essays,* and the *Dunciad* (Ian Jack). One could instance many more. Perhaps no poet ever conforms exactly to what he thinks he is doing or professes he ought to do; but the intelligent reader at least has the obligation to consider his intention and his attitude toward his art when that information is available.

The reader of Augustan poetry, especially, has to overcome the disadvantage of a whole shift in taste between Pope's day and our own. If he has failed to shed his romantic preconceptions, or if he is unfamiliar with neoclassical assumptions, he will be unable to take that poetry on its own terms; and he will miss much. Some acquaintance with critical theory would at least prevent his searching *Eloisa and Abelard* for evidence of sincerity and self-expression. What is he to make of the *Rape of the Lock* if he is ignorant of the tradition behind it and the consequent complexities of its idiom? And what better definition has ever been given of mock-heroic than Pope's own: " 'Tis using a vast force to lift a feather"? When Pope turned to criticism, it was almost always because he wished to help his readers understand his practices as a poet. It is hoped that the present collection will add to that understanding.

Note on the Text

The selections contained in this volume have been arranged according to the subjects which they discuss: pastoral poetry, epic poetry, and drama. Those pieces which do not center upon a specific genre, and which come as close as Pope ever does to statements of critical principles, have been placed in the first section, "General Theory." I have also supplied subtitles in the selections from Pope's correspondence and from his Observations on the *Iliad.*

Spelling and punctuation have been modernized for all the selections, and translations are given in the text for all quotations in a foreign language, except when the original is necessary for the point Pope is making. Unless otherwise indicated, the translations are the editor's. The original quotations are given in footnotes. The texts of the *Essay on Criticism,* the Preface to the *Works* of 1717, and the *Discourse on Pastoral Poetry* are based on those in *Pastoral Poetry and An Essay on Criticism,* ed. E. Audra and Aubrey Williams, Twickenham Edition of the Poems of Alexander Pope, Vol. I (London, 1961), and are used by permission of Methuen and Company and the Yale University Press. The selections from Pope's letters are based on the texts in *The Correspondence of Alexander Pope,* ed. George Sherburn, 5 vols. (Oxford, 1956), and are used by permission of the Clarendon Press.

All other texts are from the first editions. Those of Pope's Homeric criticism (Preface to the *Iliad,* Observations on the *Iliad,* and Postscript to the *Odyssey*) follow the folio rather than the quarto edition.

Pope's own footnotes have been retained where they are still helpful, his authorship being indicated by his name in brackets following the note. I am indebted to the editors of the Twickenham edition for the information in many of the notes to the *Essay on Criticism.* Where appropriate, I have indicated indebtedness to other editors by placing their names in parentheses following the notes.

BERTRAND A. GOLDGAR

Lawrence University, Appleton, Wisconsin

Selected Bibliography

BUTT, JOHN. *Pope's Taste in Shakespeare*. London: Oxford University Press, 1936.

CRANE, R. S. "English Neoclassical Criticism: An Outline Sketch," in *Critics and Criticism: Ancient and Modern*, ed. R. S. Crane. Chicago: University of Chicago Press, 1952.

———. "On Writing the History of English Criticism, 1650–1800," *University of Toronto Quarterly*, XXII (1953), 376–391.

HAGSTRUM, JEAN. *The Sister Arts*. Chicago: University of Chicago Press, 1958.

HOOKER, E. N. "Pope on Wit: The *Essay on Criticism*," in *The Seventeenth Century: Studies in the History of English Thought and Literature by R. F. Jones and Others*. Stanford: Stanford University Press, 1951.

JACK, IAN. *Augustan Satire: Intention and Idiom in English Poetry, 1660–1750*. Oxford: Clarendon Press, 1952.

KNIGHT, DOUGLAS. *Pope and the Heroic Tradition*. New Haven: Yale University Press, 1951.

LOVEJOY, A. O. *Essays in the History of Ideas*. New York: George Braziller, 1955.

MONK, S. H. "A Grace Beyond the Reach of Art," *Journal of the History of Ideas*, V (1944), 131–150.

———. *The Sublime*. Ann Arbor: Ann Arbor Paperbacks, Universtiy of Michigan Press, 1960.

POPE, ALEXANDER. *Pastoral Poetry and An Essay on Criticism*, ed. E. Audra and Aubrey Williams, Twickenham Edition, I. London: Methuen, 1961.

———. *Peri Bathous, or the Art of Sinking in Poetry*, ed. Edna Leake Steeves. New York: King's Crown Press, 1952.

SMITH, D. NICHOL. *Shakespeare in the Eighteenth Century*. Oxford: Clarendon Press, 1928.

ROOT, R. K. *The Poetical Career of Alexander Pope*. Princeton: Princeton University Press, 1938.

TILLOTSON, GEOFFREY. *The Poetry of Pope*. Oxford: Clarendon Press, 1938.

WARREN, AUSTIN. *Alexander Pope as Critic and Humanist*. Princeton: Princeton University Press, 1929.

GENERAL THEORY

An Essay on Criticism (1711)

PART I

Introduction. That 'tis as great a fault to judge ill as to write ill, and a more dangerous one to the public. That a true taste is as rare to be found as a true genius. That most men are born with some taste, but spoiled by false education. The multitude of critics, and causes of them. That we are to study our own taste and know the limits of it. Nature the best guide of judgment. Improved by art and rules, which are but methodized Nature. Rules derived from the practice of the ancient poets. That therefore the Ancients are necessary to be studied by a critic, particularly Homer and Virgil. Of licenses and the use of them by the Ancients. Reverence due to the Ancients, and praise of them.

'Tis hard to say, if greater want of skill
Appear in writing or in judging ill;
But, of the two, less dangerous is th' offense,
To tire our patience, than mislead our sense.
Some few in that, but numbers err in this,
Ten censure wrong for one who writes amiss;
A fool might once himself alone expose,
Now one in verse makes many more in prose.
   'Tis with our judgments as our watches, none
Go just alike, yet each believes his own.   10
In poets as true genius is but rare,
True taste as seldom is the critic's share;
Both must alike from Heaven derive their light,
These born to judge, as well as those to write.
Let such teach others who themselves excel,
And censure freely who have written well.
Authors are partial to their wit, 'tis true,
But are not critics to their judgment too?
   Yet if we look more closely, we shall find
Most have the seeds of judgment in their mind;   20
Nature affords at least a glimmering light;
The lines, though touched but faintly, are drawn right.
But as the slightest sketch, if justly traced,
Is by ill coloring but the more disgraced,

3

So by false learning is good sense defaced;
Some are bewildered in the maze of schools,
And some made coxcombs nature meant but fools.
In search of wit these lose their common sense,
And then turn critics in their own defense.
Each burns alike, who can, or cannot write,   30
Or with a rival's, or an eunuch's spite.
All fools have still an itching to deride,
And fain would be upon the laughing side:
If Maevius[1] scribble in Apollo's spite,
There are, who judge still worse than he can write.
    Some have at first for wits, then poets passed,
Turned critics next, and proved plain fools at last;
Some neither can for wits nor critics pass,
As heavy mules are neither horse nor ass.
Those half-learned witlings, numerous in our isle,   40
As half-formed insects on the banks of Nile;
Unfinished things, one knows not what to call,
Their generation's so equivocal:[2]
To tell[3] 'em, would a hundred tongues require,
Or one vain wit's, that might a hundred tire.
    But you who seek to give and merit fame,
And justly bear a critic's noble name,
Be sure yourself and your own reach to know,
How far your genius, taste, and learning go;
Launch not beyond your depth, but be discreet,   50
And mark that point where sense and dullness meet.
    Nature to all things fixed the limits fit,
And wisely curbed proud man's pretending wit.
As on the land while here the ocean gains,
In other parts it leaves wide sandy plains;
Thus in the soul while memory prevails,
The solid power of understanding fails;
Where beams of warm imagination play,
The memory's soft figures melt away.
One science only will one genius fit;   60
So vast is art, so narrow human wit:
Not only bounded to peculiar arts,
But oft in those, confined to single parts.
Like kings we lose the conquests gained before,

1. An inferior poet alluded to by Virgil and Horace.
2. Equivocal generation: the supposed spontaneous generation of plants and animals.
3. Count.

By vain ambition still to make them more:
Each might his several province well command,
Would all but stoop to what they understand.
    First follow Nature, and your judgment frame
By her just standard, which is still⁴ the same:
Unerring Nature, still divinely bright,   70
One clear, unchanged, and universal light,
Life, force, and beauty, must to all impart,
At once the source, and end, and test of art.
Art from that fund each just supply provides,
Works without show, and without pomp presides:
In some fair body thus th' informing soul
With spirits feeds, with vigor fills the whole,
Each motion guides, and every nerve sustains;
Itself unseen, but in th' effects, remains.
Some, to whom Heaven in wit has been profuse,   80
Want as much more, to turn it to its use;
For wit and judgment often are at strife,
Though meant each other's aid, like man and wife.
'Tis more to guide than spur the Muse's steed;
Restrain his fury, than provoke his speed;
The winged courser, like a generous⁵ horse,
Shows most true mettle when you check his course.
    Those rules of old discovered, not devised,
Are Nature still, but Nature methodized;
Nature, like liberty, is but restrained   90
By the same laws which first herself ordained.
    Hear how learned Greece her useful rules indites,
When to repress, and when indulge our flights:
High on Parnassus' top her sons she showed,
And pointed out those arduous paths they trod,
Held from afar, aloft, th' immortal prize,
And urged the rest by equal steps to rise;
Just precepts thus from great examples given,
She drew from them what they derived from Heaven.
The generous critic fanned the poet's fire,   100
And taught the world with reason to admire.
Then Criticism the Muse's handmaid proved,
To dress her charms, and make her more beloved;
But following wits from that intention strayed;
Who could not win the mistress, wooed the maid;
Against the poets their own arms they turned,

4. Always.
5. Spirited.

Sure to hate most the men from whom they learned.
So modern 'pothecaries, taught the art
By doctor's bills[6] to play the doctor's part,
Bold in the practice of mistaken rules,   110
Prescribe, apply, and call their masters fools.
Some on the leaves of ancient authors prey,
Nor time nor moths e'er spoiled so much as they;
Some dryly plain, without invention's aid,
Write dull receipts how poems may be made;
These leave the sense, their learning to display,
And those explain the meaning quite away.
    You then whose judgment the right course would steer,
Know well each Ancient's proper character,
His fable, subject, scope in every page,   120
Religion, country, genius of his age:
Without all these at once before your eyes,
Cavil you may, but never criticize.
Be Homer's works your study and delight,
Read them by day, and meditate by night;
Thence form your judgment, thence your maxims bring,
And trace the Muses upward to their spring.
Still with itself compared, his text peruse;
And let your comment be the Mantuan Muse.[7]
    When first young Maro[8] in his boundless mind   130
A work t' outlast immortal Rome designed,
Perhaps he seemed above the critic's law,
And but from Nature's fountains scorned to draw:
But when t' examine every part he came,
Nature and Homer were, he found, the same.
Convinced, amazed, he checks the bold design,
And rules as strict his labored work confine,
As if the Stagirite[9] o'erlooked each line.
Learn hence for ancient rules a just esteem;
To copy Nature is to copy them.   140
    Some beauties yet no precepts can declare,
For there's a happiness as well as care.
Music resembles poetry, in each
Are nameless graces which no methods teach,
And which a master hand alone can reach.
If, where the rules not far enough extend,

6. Prescriptions.
7. Virgil.
8. Virgil.
9. Aristotle.

(Since rules were made but to promote their end)
Some lucky license answers to the full
Th' intent proposed, that license is a rule.
Thus Pegasus, a nearer way to take,   150
May boldly deviate from the common track.
Great wits sometimes may gloriously offend,
And rise to faults true critics dare not mend;
From vulgar bounds with brave disorder part,
And snatch a grace beyond the reach of art,
Which, without passing through the judgment, gains
The heart, and all its end at once attains.
In prospects, thus, some objects please our eyes,
Which out of Nature's common order rise,
The shapeless rock, or hanging precipice.   160
But though the Ancients thus their rules invade,
(As kings dispense with laws themselves have made)
Moderns, beware! Or if you must offend
Against the precept, ne'er transgress its end;
Let it be seldom, and compelled by need,
And have, at least, their precedent to plead.
The critic else proceeds without remorse,
Seizes your fame, and puts his laws in force.
    I know there are, to whose presumptuous thoughts
Those freer beauties, even in them, seem faults.   170
Some figures monstrous and misshaped appear,
Considered singly, or beheld too near,
Which, but proportioned to their light, or place,
Due distance reconciles to form and grace.
A prudent chief not always must display
His powers in equal ranks, and fair array,
But with th' occasion and the place comply,
Conceal his force, nay seem sometimes to fly.
Those oft are stratagems which errors seem,
Nor is it Homer nods, but we that dream.   180
    Still green with bays each ancient altar stands,
Above the reach of sacrilegious hands,
Secure from flames, from envy's fiercer rage,
Destructive war, and all-involving age.
See, from each clime the learned their incense bring!
Hear, in all tongues consenting[10] paeans ring!
In praise so just, let every voice be joined,
And fill the general chorus of mankind!
Hail, bards triumphant! born in happier days;

10. Harmonious.

8 LITERARY CRITICISM OF POPE

Immortal heirs of universal praise! 190
Whose honors with increase of ages grow,
As streams roll down, enlarging as they flow!
Nations unborn your mighty names shall sound,
And worlds applaud that must not yet be found!
Oh may some spark of your celestial fire
The last, the meanest of your sons inspire,
(That on weak wings, from far, pursues your flights;
Glows while he reads, but trembles as he writes)
To teach vain wits a science little known,
T' admire superior sense, and doubt their own! 200

PART II

Causes hindering a true judgment. 1. Pride. 2. Imperfect learning.
3. Judging by parts, and not by the whole. Critics in wit, language,
versification, only. 4. Being too hard to please, or too apt to admire.
5. Partiality—too much love to a sect—to the Ancients or Moderns. 6.
Prejudice or prevention. 7. Singularity. 8. Inconstancy. 9. Party spirit.
10. Envy. Against envy and in praise of good nature. When severity is
chiefly to be used by critics.

Of all the causes which conspire to blind
Man's erring judgment, and misguide the mind,
What the weak head with strongest bias rules,
Is pride, the never-failing vice of fools.
Whatever Nature has in worth denied,
She gives in large recruits[11] of needful pride;
For as in bodies, thus in souls, we find
What wants in blood and spirits, swelled with wind;
Pride, where wit fails, steps in to our defense,
And fills up all the mighty void of sense. 210
If once right reason drives that cloud away,
Truth breaks upon us with resistless day;
Trust not yourself; but your defects to know,
Make use of every friend—and every foe.
A little learning is a dangerous thing;
Drink deep, or taste not the Pierian spring:[12]
There shallow draughts intoxicate the brain,
And drinking largely sobers us again.
Fired at first sight with what the Muse imparts,
In fearless youth we tempt the heights of arts, 220

11. Additional supplies.
12. Spring sacred to the Muses.

While from the bounded level of our mind,
Short views we take, nor see the lengths behind;
But more advanced, behold with strange surprise
New, distant scenes of endless science[13] rise!
So pleased at first the towering Alps we try,
Mount o'er the vales, and seem to tread the sky;
Th' eternal snows appear already passed,
And the first clouds and mountains seem the last:
But those attained, we tremble to survey
The growing labors of the lengthened way,   230
Th' increasing prospect tires our wandering eyes,
Hills peep o'er hills, and Alps on Alps arise!
    A perfect judge will read each work of wit
With the same spirit that its author writ,
Survey the whole, nor seek slight faults to find,
Where Nature moves, and rapture warms the mind;
Nor lose, for that malignant dull delight,
The generous pleasure to be charmed with wit.
But in such lays as neither ebb, nor flow,
Correctly cold, and regularly low,   240
That shunning faults, one quiet tenor keep;
We cannot blame indeed—but we may sleep.
In wit, as Nature, what affects our hearts
Is not th' exactness of peculiar parts;
'Tis not a lip, or eye, we beauty call,
But the joint force and full result of all.
Thus when we view some well-proportioned dome,
(The world's just wonder, and even thine, O Rome!)
No single parts unequally surprise;
All comes united to th' admiring eyes;   250
No monstrous height, or breadth, or length appear;
The whole at once is bold, and regular.
    Whoever thinks a faultless piece to see,
Thinks what ne'er was, nor is, nor e'er shall be.
In every work regard the writer's end,
Since none can compass more than they intend;
And if the means be just, the conduct true,
Applause, in spite of trivial faults, is due.
As men of breeding, sometimes men of wit,
T' avoid great errors, must the less commit,   260
Neglect the rules each verbal critic lays,[14]
For not to know some trifles, is a praise.

13. Knowledge.
14. Verbal critic: one excessively concerned with the details of the text.

Most critics, fond of some subservient art,
Still make the whole depend upon a part;
They talk of principles, but notions prize,
And all to one loved folly sacrifice.
Once on a time, La Mancha's knight, they say,[15]
A certain bard encountering on the way,
Discoursed in terms as just, with looks as sage,
As e'er could Dennis[16] of the Grecian stage;   270
Concluding all were desperate sots and fools,
Who durst depart from Aristotle's rules.
Our author, happy in a judge so nice,
Produced his play, and begged the knight's advice,
Made him observe the subject and the plot,
The manners, passions, unities, what not?
All which, exact to rule were brought about,
Were but a combat in the lists left out.
"What! Leave the combat out?" exclaims the knight;
Yes, or we must renounce the Stagirite.   280
"Not so, by Heaven" (he answers in a rage)
"Knights, squires, and steeds, must enter on the stage."
So vast a throng the stage can ne'er contain.
"Then build a new, or act it in a plain."
        Thus critics, of less judgment than caprice,
Curious, not knowing, not exact, but nice,
Form short ideas; and offend in arts
(As most in manners) by a love to parts.
        Some to conceit alone their taste confine,
And glittering thoughts struck out at every line;   290
Pleased with a work where nothing's just or fit;
One glaring chaos and wild heap of wit.
Poets like painters, thus, unskilled to trace
The naked nature and the living grace,
With gold and jewels cover every part,
And hide with ornaments their want of art.
True wit is Nature to advantage dressed,
What oft was thought, but ne'er so well expressed;
Something, whose truth convinced at sight we find,
That gives us back the image of our mind.   300
As shades more sweetly recommend the light,
So modest plainness sets off sprightly wit.
For works may have more wit than does 'em good,

15. La Mancha's knight: Don Quixote; the episode is from Avellaneda's
spurious sequel to *Don Quixote*.
    16. John Dennis, contemporary critic; see the note to l. 585.

As bodies perish through excess of blood.
    Others for language all their care express,
And value books, as women men, for dress;
Their praise is still—the style is excellent:
The sense, they humbly take upon content.[17]
Words are like leaves; and where they most abound,
Much fruit of sense beneath is rarely found.   310
False eloquence, like the prismatic glass,
Its gaudy colors spreads on every place;
The face of Nature we no more survey,
All glares alike, without distinction gay:
But true expression, like th' unchanging sun,
Clears, and improves whate'er it shines upon,
It gilds all objects, but it alters none.
Expression is the dress of thought, and still
Appears more decent as more suitable;
A vile conceit in pompous words expressed,   320
Is like a clown in regal purple dressed;
For different styles with different subjects sort,
As several garbs with country, town, and court.
Some by old words to fame have made pretense,
Ancients in phrase, mere Moderns in their sense.
Such labored nothings, in so strange a style,
Amaze th'unlearned, and make the learned smile.
Unlucky, as Fungoso in the play,[18]
These sparks with awkward vanity display
What the fine gentleman wore yesterday;   330
And but so mimic ancient wits at best,
As apes our grandsires in their doublets dressed.
In words, as fashions, the same rule will hold:
Alike fantastic, if too new, or old;
Be not the first by whom the new are tried,
Nor yet the last to lay the old aside.
    But most by numbers judge a poet's song,
And smooth or rough, with them, is right or wrong;
In the bright Muse though thousand charms conspire,
Her voice is all these tuneful fools admire,   340
Who haunt Parnassus but to please their ear,
Not mend their minds; as some to church repair,
Not for the doctrine, but the music there.
These equal syllables alone require,
Tho' oft the ear the open vowels tire;

17. Accept unquestioningly.
18. In Ben Jonson's *Every Man Out of His Humour.*

While expletives their feeble aid *do* join,
And ten low words oft creep in one dull line;
While they ring round the same unvaried chimes,
With sure returns of still expected rhymes,
Where'er you find "the cooling western breeze,"   350
In the next line, it "whispers through the trees";
If crystal streams with "pleasing murmurs creep,"
The reader's threatened (not in vain) with "sleep."
Then, at the last, and only couplet fraught
With some unmeaning thing they call a thought,
A needless alexandrine ends the song,
That like a wounded snake, drags its slow length along.
Leave such to tune their own dull rhymes, and know
What's roundly smooth, or languishingly slow;
And praise the easy vigor of a line,   360
Where Denham's strength, and Waller's sweetness join.[19]
True ease in writing comes from art, not chance,
As those move easiest who have learned to dance.
'Tis not enough no harshness gives offence,
The sound must seem an echo to the sense.
Soft is the strain when Zephyr gently blows,
And the smooth stream in smoother numbers flows;
But when loud surges lash the sounding shore,
The hoarse, rough verse should like the torrent roar.
When Ajax strives, some rock's vast weight to throw,   370
The line too labors, and the words move slow;
Not so, when swift Camilla scours the plain,
Flies o'er th' unbending corn, and skims along the main.[20]
Hear how Timotheus'[21] varied lays surprise,
And bid alternate passions fall and rise!
While, at each change, the son of Libyan Jove[22]
Now burns with glory, and then melts with love;
Now his fierce eyes with sparkling fury glow;
Now sighs steal out, and tears begin to flow:
Persians and Greeks like turns of nature found,   380
And the world's victor stood subdued by sound!
The power of music all our hearts allow;
And what Timotheus was, is Dryden now.

19. Sir John Denham (1615–1669) and Edmund Waller (1606–1687).
20. Pope's illustrative couplet imitates Virgil's description of Camilla, *Aeneid*, VII, 808–809.
21. See *Alexander's Feast, or the Power of Music,* an ode by Mr. Dryden [Pope].
22. Alexander.

Avoid extremes; and shun the fault of such,
Who still are pleased too little, or too much.
At every trifle scorn to take offence,
That always shows great pride, or little sense;
Those heads as stomachs are not sure the best
Which nauseate all, and nothing can digest.
Yet let not each gay turn thy rapture move,   390
For fools admire, but men of sense approve;
As things seem large which we through mists descry,
Dullness is ever apt to magnify.
    Some foreign writers, some our own despise;
The Ancients only, or the Moderns prize:
(Thus wit, like faith, by each man is applied
To one small sect, and all are damned beside.)
Meanly they seek the blessing to confine,
And force that sun but on a part to shine,
Which not alone the southern wit sublimes,   400
But ripens spirits in cold northern climes;
Which from the first has shone on ages past,
Enlights the present, and shall warm the last;
(Though each may feel increases and decays,
And see now clearer and now darker days)
Regard not then if wit be old or new,
But blame the false, and value still the true.
    Some ne'er advance a judgment of their own,
But catch the spreading notion of the town;
They reason and conclude by precedent,   410
And own stale nonsense which they ne'er invent.
Some judge of authors' names, not works, and then
Nor praise nor blame the writings, but the men.
Of all this servile herd the worst is he
That in proud dullness joins with quality,
A constant critic at the great man's board,
To fetch and carry nonsense for my lord.
What woeful stuff this madrigal would be,
In some starved hackney sonneteer, or me?
But let a lord once own the happy lines,   420
How the wit brightens! How the style refines!
Before his sacred name flies every fault,
And each exalted stanza teems with thought!
    The vulgar thus through imitation err;
As oft the learned by being singular;
So much they scorn the crowd, that if the throng
By chance go right, they purposely go wrong;
So schismatics the plain believers quit,

And are but damned for having too much wit.
    Some praise at morning what they blame at night;   430
But always think the last opinion right.
A Muse by these is like a mistress used,
This hour she's idolized, the next abused,
While their weak heads, like towns unfortified,
'Twixt sense and nonsense daily change their side.
Ask them the cause; they're wiser still, they say;
And still tomorrow's wiser than today.
We think our fathers fools, so wise we grow;
Our wiser sons, no doubt, will think us so.
Once school-divines this zealous isle o'erspread;   440
Who knew most sentences[23] was deepest read;
Faith, Gospel, all, seemed made to be disputed,
And none had sense enough to be confuted.
Scotists and Thomists, now, in peace remain,
Amidst their kindred cobwebs in Duck Lane.[24]
If faith itself has different dresses worn,
What wonder modes in wit should take their turn?
Oft, leaving what is natural and fit,
The current folly proves the ready wit,
And authors think their reputation safe,   450
Which lives as long as fools are pleased to laugh.
    Some valuing those of their own side, or mind,
Still make themselves the measure of mankind;
Fondly we think we honor merit then,
When we but praise ourselves in other men.
Parties in wit attend on those of state,
And public faction doubles private hate.
Pride, malice, folly, against Dryden rose,
In various shapes of parsons, critics, beaus;
But sense survived, when merry jests were past;   460
For rising merit will buoy up at last.
Might he return, and bless once more our eyes,
New Blackmores and new Milbourns[25] must arise;
Nay, should great Homer lift his awful head,
Zoilus[26] again would start up from the dead.
Envy will merit as its shade pursue,

23. Theological maxims.
24. A place where old and second-hand books were sold formerly, near Smithfield [Pope].
25. Sir Richard Blackmore was one of the "critics" and Luke Milbourn one of the "parsons" who attacked Dryden.
26. A Greek grammarian who attacked Homer.

But like a shadow, proves the substance true;
For envied wit, like Sol eclipsed, makes known
Th' opposing body's grossness, not its own.
When first that sun too powerful beams displays,   470
It draws up vapors which obscure its rays;
But even those clouds at last adorn its way,
Reflect new glories, and augment the day.
    Be thou the first true merit to befriend;
His praise is lost, who stays till all commend;
Short is the date, alas, of modern rhymes;
And 'tis but just to let them live betimes.
No longer now that Golden Age appears,
When patriarch wits survived a thousand years;
Now length of fame (our second life) is lost,   480
And bare threescore is all even that can boast;
Our sons their fathers' failing language see,
And such as Chaucer is, shall Dryden be.
So when the faithful pencil has designed
Some bright idea of the master's mind,
Where a new world leaps out at his command,
And ready Nature waits upon his hand;
When the ripe colors soften and unite,
And sweetly melt into just shade and light,
When mellowing years their full perfection give,   490
And each bold figure just begins to live;
The treacherous colors the fair art betray,
And all the bright creation fades away!
    Unhappy wit, like most mistaken things,
Atones not for that envy which it brings.
In youth alone its empty praise we boast,
But soon the short-lived vanity is lost!
Like some fair flower the early spring supplies,
That gaily blooms, but even in blooming dies.
What is this wit which must our cares employ?   500
The owner's wife, that other men enjoy;
Then most our trouble still when most admired,
And still the more we give, the more required;
Whose fame with pains we guard, but lose with ease,
Sure some to vex, but never all to please;
'Tis what the vicious fear, the virtuous shun;
By fools 'tis hated, and by knaves undone!
    If wit so much from ignorance undergo,
Ah, let not learning too commence its foe!
Of old, those met rewards who could excel,   510

And such were praised who but endeavored well:
Though triumphs were to generals only due,
Crowns were reserved to grace the soldiers too.
Now, they who reach Parnassus' lofty crown,
Employ their pains to spurn some others down;
And while self-love each jealous writer rules,
Contending wits become the sport of fools.
But still the worst with most regret commend,
For each ill author is as bad a friend.
To what base ends, and by what abject ways,   520
Are mortals urged through sacred[27] lust of praise!
Ah, ne'er so dire a thirst of glory boast,
Nor in the critic let the man be lost!
Good nature and good sense must ever join;
To err is human, to forgive, divine.

But if in noble minds some dregs remain,
Not yet purged off, of spleen and sour disdain,
Discharge that rage on more provoking crimes,
Nor fear a dearth in these flagitious times.
No pardon vile obscenity should find,   530
Though wit and art conspire to move your mind;
But dullness with obscenity must prove
As shameful sure as impotence in love.
In the fat age of pleasure, wealth, and ease,[28]
Sprung the rank weed, and thrived with large increase;
When love was all an easy monarch's care;
Seldom at council, never in a war:
Jilts ruled the state, and statesmen farces writ;
Nay, wits had pensions, and young lords had wit:
The fair sat panting at a courtier's play,   540
And not a mask[29] went unimproved away:
The modest fan was lifted up no more,
And virgins smiled at what they blushed before.
The following license of a foreign reign[30]
Did all the dregs of bold Socinus[31] drain;
Then unbelieving priests reformed the nation,
And taught more pleasant methods of salvation;
Where Heaven's free subjects might their rights dispute,

27. Accursed.
28. I.e., the age of Charles II.
29. Any woman wearing a vizard mask to the theater, but often used
to mean prostitute.
30. That of William III.
31. Sixteenth-century theologian who denied the divinity of Christ.

Lest God himself should seem too absolute.
Pulpits their sacred satire learned to spare,   550
And Vice admired to find a flatterer there!
Encouraged thus, wit's Titans braved the skies,[32]
And the press groaned with licensed blasphemies.
These monsters, critics! with your darts engage,
Here point your thunder, and exhaust your rage!
Yet shun their fault, who, scandalously nice,
Will needs mistake an author into vice;
All seems infected that th' infected spy,
As all looks yellow to the jaundiced eye.

PART III

Rules for the conduct of manners in a critic. 1. Candor, modesty, good breeding, sincerity, and freedom of advice. 2. When one's counsel is to be restrained. Character of an incorrigible poet. And of an impertinent critic. Character of a good critic. The history of criticism and characters of the best critics: Aristotle, Horace, Dionysius, Petronius, Quintilian, Longinus. Of the decay of criticism and its revival. Erasmus, Vida, Boileau, Lord Roscommon, etc. Conclusion.

Learn then what morals critics ought to show,   560
For 'tis but half a judge's task, to know.
'Tis not enough, taste, judgment, learning, join;
In all you speak, let truth and candor shine:
That not alone what to your sense is due,
All may allow; but seek your friendship too.
    Be silent always when you doubt your sense;
And speak, though sure, with seeming diffidence:
Some positive persisting fops we know,
Who, if once wrong, will needs be always so;
But you, with pleasure own your errors past,   570
And make each day a critic[33] on the last.
    'Tis not enough your counsel still be true;
Blunt truths more mischief than nice falsehoods do;
Men must be taught as if you taught them not;
And things unknown proposed as things forgot.
Without good breeding, truth is disapproved;
That only makes superior sense beloved.
    Be niggards of advice on no pretense;
For the worst avarice is that of sense.

32. Pope refers to deists and other freethinkers.
33. A critique or criticism.

With mean complacence ne'er betray your trust,   580
Nor be so civil as to prove unjust;
Fear not the anger of the wise to raise;
Those best can bear reproof, who merit praise.
    'Twere well, might critics still this freedom take;
But Appius[34] reddens at each word you speak,
And stares, tremendous, with a threatening eye,
Like some fierce tyrant in old tapestry!
Fear most to tax an honorable fool,[35]
Whose right it is, uncensured to be dull;
Such without wit are poets when they please,   590
As without learning they can take degrees.[36]
Leave dangerous truths to unsuccessful satires,
And flattery to fulsome dedicators,
Whom, when they praise, the world believes no more,
Than when they promise to give scribbling o'er.
'Tis best sometimes your censure to restrain,
And charitably let the dull be vain:
Your silence there is better than your spite,
For who can rail so long as they can write?
Still humming on, their drowsy course they keep,   600
And lashed so long, like tops, are lashed asleep.[37]
False steps but help them to renew the race,
As, after stumbling, jades will mend their pace.
What crowds of these, impenitently bold,
In sounds and jingling syllables grown old,
Still run on poets in a raging vein,
Even to the dregs and squeezings of the brain,
Strain out the last, dull droppings of their sense,
And rhyme with all the rage of impotence!
    Such shameless bards we have; and yet 'tis true,   610
There are as mad, abandoned critics too.
The bookful blockhead, ignorantly read,
With loads of learned lumber in his head,
With his own tongue still edifies his ears,

34. This picture was taken to himself by John Dennis, a furious old critic by profession, who, upon no other provocation, wrote against this Essay and its author in a manner perfectly lunatic; for, as to the mention made of him in ver. 270, he took it as a compliment and said it was treacherously meant to cause him to overlook this abuse of his person [Pope].

35. A foolish nobleman.

36. Unearned degrees could be conferred upon noblemen.

37. A top was said to "sleep" when spinning so fast that its motion could hardly be seen.

And always listening to himself appears.
All books he reads, and all he reads assails,
From Dryden's Fables down to Durfey's Tales.[38]
With him, most authors steal their works, or buy;
Garth did not write his own *Dispensary*.[39]
Name a new play, and he's the poet's friend,   620
Nay, showed his faults—but when would poets mend?
No place so sacred from such fops is barred,
Nor is Paul's church more safe than Paul's church-yard:[40]
Nay, fly to altars; there they'll talk you dead;
For fools rush in where angels fear to tread.
Distrustful sense with modest caution speaks;
It still looks home, and short excursions makes;
But rattling nonsense in full volleys breaks;
And never shocked, and never turned aside,
Bursts out, resistless, with a thundering tide!   630
     But where's the man, who counsel can bestow,
Still pleased to teach, and yet not proud to know?
Unbiased, or by favor or by spite;
Not dully prepossessed, nor blindly right;
Though learned, well-bred; and though well-bred, sincere;
Modestly bold, and humanly severe?
Who to a friend his faults can freely show,
And gladly praise the merit of a foe?
Blest with a taste exact, yet unconfined;
A knowledge both of books and human kind;   640
Generous converse; a soul exempt from pride;
And love to praise, with reason on his side?
     Such once were critics, such the happy few,
Athens and Rome in better ages knew.
The mighty Stagirite first left the shore,
Spread all his sails, and durst the deeps explore;
He steered securely, and discovered far,
Led by the light of the Maeonian star.[41]
Poets, a race long unconfined and free,
Still fond and proud of savage liberty,   650
Received his laws, and stood convinced 'twas fit
Who conquered Nature, should preside o'er wit.
     Horace still charms with graceful negligence,

38. Thomas D'Urfey (1653–1723).
39. A common slander at that time in prejudice of that deserving author [Pope]. Sir Samuel Garth's mock-epic appeared in 1699.
40. The booksellers' quarter.
41. Homer.

And without method talks us into sense,
Will like a friend familiarly convey
The truest notions in the easiest way.
He, who supreme in judgment, as in wit,
Might boldly censure, as he boldly writ,
Yet judged with coolness though he sung with fire;
His precepts teach but what his works inspire.   660
Our critics take a contrary extreme,
They judge with fury, but they write with phlegm:
Nor suffers Horace more in wrong translations
By wits, than critics in as wrong quotations.[42]
    See Dionysius[43] Homer's thoughts refine,
And call new beauties forth from every line!
    Fancy and art in gay Petronius[44] please,
The scholar's learning, with the courtier's ease.
    In grave Quintilian's copious work we find
The justest rules, and clearest method joined;   670
Thus useful arms in magazines we place,
All ranged in order, and disposed with grace,
But less to please the eye, than arm the hand,
Still fit for use, and ready at command.
    Thee, bold Longinus! all the Nine inspire,
And bless their critic with a poet's fire.
An ardent judge, who zealous in his trust,
With warmth gives sentence, yet is always just;
Whose own example strengthens all his laws,
And is himself that great sublime he draws.   680
    Thus long succeeding critics justly reigned,
License repressed, and useful laws ordained;
Learning and Rome alike in empire grew,
And arts still followed where her eagles flew;
From the same foes, at last, both felt their doom,
And the same age saw learning fall, and Rome.
With tyranny, then superstition joined,
As that the body, this enslaved the mind;
Much was believed, but little understood,
And to be dull was construed to be good;   690
A second deluge learning thus o'errun,
And the monks finished what the Goths begun.
    At length, Erasmus, that great injured name,

42. I.e., than *by* critics in as wrong quotations.
43. Dionysius of Halicarnassus, Greek critic of the first century B.C.
44. Author of the *Satyricon*, which contains some scattered criticism.

(The glory of the priesthood, and the shame!)[45]
Stemmed the wild torrent of a barbarous age,
And drove those holy vandals off the stage.
   But see! each Muse, in Leo's[46] golden days,
Starts from her trance, and trims her withered bays!
Rome's ancient Genius, o'er its ruins spread,
Shakes off the dust, and rears his reverend head!   700
Then sculptuie and her sister arts revive;
Stones leaped to form, and rocks began to live;
With sweeter notes each rising temple rung;
A Raphael painted, and a Vida[47] sung.
Immortal Vida! on whose honored brow
The poet's bays and critic's ivy grow:
Cremona now shall ever boast thy name,
As next in place to Mantua, next in fame![48]
   But soon by impious arms from Latium chased,[49]
Their ancient bounds the banished Muses passed;   710
Thence arts o'er all the northern world advance;
But critic learning flourished most in France.
The rules, a nation born to serve, obeys;
And Boileau[50] still in right of Horace sways.
But we, brave Britons, foreign laws despised,
And kept unconquered, and uncivilized;
Fierce for the liberties of wit, and bold,
We still defied the Romans, as of old.
Yet some there were, among the sounder few
Of those who less presumed, and better knew,   720
Who durst assert the juster ancient cause,
And here restored wit's fundamental laws.
Such was the Muse,[51] whose rules and practice tell,
"Nature's chief masterpiece is writing well."
Such was Roscommon,[52] not more learned than good,
With manners generous as his noble blood;

45. Pope alludes to the persecution of Erasmus by the Church.
46. Leo X, Pope from 1513 to 1521 and patron of the arts.
47. M. Hieronymus Vida, an excellent Latin poet who writ an *Art of Poetry* in verse. He flourished in the time of Leo X [Pope].
48. Cremona is the birthplace of Vida, Mantua of Virgil.
49. The sack of Rome in 1527 by the Duke of Bourbon.
50. Boileau's *L'Art Poétique* (1674) imitates Horace's *Ars Poetica*.
51. John Sheffield, third Earl of Mulgrave, Duke of Buckingham, from whose *Essay on Poetry* (1682) Pope quotes.
52. Wentworth Dillon, Earl of Roscommon, author of an *Essay on Translated Verse* (1684).

To him the wit of Greece and Rome was known,
And every author's merit, but his own.
Such late was Walsh—the Muse's judge and friend,[53]
Who justly knew to blame or to commend;   730
To failings mild, but zealous for desert;
The clearest head and the sincerest heart.
This humble praise, lamented shade! receive,
This praise at least a grateful Muse may give!
The Muse, whose early voice you taught to sing,
Prescribed her heights, and pruned her tender wing,
(Her guide now lost) no more attempts to rise,
But in low numbers short excursions tries:
Content, if hence th' unlearned their wants may view,
The learned reflect on what before they knew: 740
Careless of censure, nor too fond of fame,
Still pleased to praise, yet not afraid to blame,
Averse alike to flatter, or offend;
Not free from faults, nor yet too vain to mend.

53. William Walsh (1663–1708), poet, critic, and literary mentor of Pope's early years.

Preface to the *Works* of 1717

I am inclined to think that both the writers of books and the readers of them are generally not a little unreasonable in their expectations. The first seem to fancy that the world must approve whatever they produce and the latter to imagine that authors are obliged to please them at any rate. Methinks as, on the one hand, no single man is born with a right of controlling the opinions of all the rest, so, on the other, the world has no title to demand that the whole care and time of any particular person should be sacrificed to its entertainment. Therefore I cannot but believe that writers and readers are under equal obligations for as much fame or pleasure as each affords the other.

Everyone acknowledges it would be a wild notion to expect perfection in any work of man; and yet one would think the contrary was taken for granted by the judgment commonly passed upon poems. A critic supposes he has done his part if he proves a writer to have failed in an expression or erred in any particular point; and can it then be wondered at if the poets in general seem resolved not to own themselves in any error? For as long as one side will make no allowances, the other will be brought to no acknowledgements.

I am afraid this extreme zeal on both sides is ill placed, poetry and criticism being by no means the universal concern of the world but only the affair of idle men who write in their closets and of idle men who read there.

Yet sure, upon the whole, a bad author deserves better usage than a bad critic; for a writer's endeavor, for the most part, is to please his readers, and he fails merely through the misfortune of an ill judgment; but such a critic's is to put them out of humor, a design he could never go upon without both that and an ill temper.

I think a good deal may be said to extenuate the fault of bad poets. What we call a genius is hard to be distinguished by a man himself from a strong inclination; and if his genius be ever so great, he can not at first discover it any other way than by giving way to that prevalent propensity which renders him the more liable to be mistaken. The only method he has is to make the experiment by writing and appealing to the judgment of others; now, if he happens to write ill (which is certainly no sin in itself) he is immediately made an object of ridicule. I wish we had the humanity to reflect that even the worst authors might, in their endeavor to please us, deserve something at our hands. We have no cause to quarrel with them but for their obstinacy in persisting to write; and this too may admit of alleviating circumstances. Their particular friends may be either ignorant or insincere; and the rest of the world in general is too well bred to shock them with a truth which generally their booksellers are the first that inform them of. This happens not till they have spent too much of their time to apply to any profession which might better fit their talents, and till such talents as they have are so far discredited as to be but of small service to them. For (what is the hardest case imaginable) the reputation of a man generally depends upon the first steps he makes in the world, and people will establish their opinion of us from what we do at that season when we have least judgment to direct us.

On the other hand, a good poet no sooner communicates his works with the same desire of information but it is imagined he is a vain young creature given up to the ambition of fame, when perhaps the poor man is all the while trembling with the fear of being ridiculous. If he is made to hope he may please the world, he falls under very unlucky circumstances; for, from the moment he prints, he must expect to hear no more truth than if he were a prince or a beauty. If he has not very good sense (and indeed there are twenty men of wit for one man of sense), his living thus in a course of flattery may put him in no small danger of becoming a coxcomb; if he has, he will consequently have so much diffidence as not to reap any great satisfaction from his praise, since if it be given to his face it can scarce be distinguished from flattery, and if in his absence it is hard to be certain of it. Were he sure to be commended by the best and most knowing, he is as sure of being envied by the worst and most ignorant, which are the majority; for it is with a fine genius as with a fine fashion, all those are displeased at it who are not able to follow it. And 'tis to be feared that esteem will seldom do any man so much good as ill-will does him harm. Then there is a third class of people who make the largest part of mankind, those of ordinary or indifferent capacities; and these (to a man) will hate or suspect him: a hundred honest gentlemen will dread him as a wit and a hundred innocent women as a satirist. In a word, whatever be his fate in poetry, it is ten to one but he must give up all the reasonable aims of life for it. There are indeed some advantages accruing from a genius to poetry, and they are all I can think of: the agreeable power of self-amusement when a man is idle or alone; the privilege of being admitted into the best company; and the freedom of saying as many careless things as other people without being so severely remarked upon.

I believe if anyone early in his life should contemplate the dangerous fate of authors, he would scarce be of their number on any consideration. The life of a wit is a warfare upon earth; and the present spirit of the learned world is such that to attempt to serve it (any way) one must have the constancy of a martyr and a resolution to suffer for its sake. I could wish people would believe what I am pretty certain they will not, that I have been less concerned about fame than I durst declare till this occasion, when methinks I should find more credit than I could heretofore, since my writings have had their fate already and 'tis too late to think of prepossessing the reader in their favor. I would plead it as some merit in me that the world has never been prepared for these trifles by prefaces, biased by recommendations, dazzled with the names of great patrons, wheedled with fine reasons and pretences, or troubled with excuses. I confess it was want of consideration that made me an author; I writ because it amused me; I corrected because it was as pleasant to me to correct as to write; and I published because I was told I might please such as it was a credit to please. To what degree I have done this, I am really ignorant; I had too much fondness for my productions to judge of them at first, and too much judgment to be pleased with them at last. But I have reason to think they can have no reputation which will continue long or which deserves to do so; for they have always fallen short not only of what I read of others but even of my own ideas of poetry.

If anyone should imagine I am not in earnest, I desire him to reflect that the Ancients (to say the least of them) had as much genius as we; and that to take more pains and employ more time cannot fail to produce more complete pieces. They constantly applied themselves not only to that art, but to that single branch of an art, to which their talent was most powerfully bent; and it was the business of their lives to correct and finish their works for posterity. If we can pretend to have used the same industry, let us expect the same immortality; though if we took the same care, we should still lie under a farther misfortune: they writ in languages that became universal and everlasting, while ours are extremely limited both in extent and in duration. A mighty foundation for our pride! when the utmost we can hope is but to be read in one island and to be thrown aside at the end of one age.

All that is left us is to recommend our productions by the imitation of the Ancients; and it will be found true that in every age the highest character for sense and learning has been obtained by those who have been most indebted to them. For to say truth, whatever is very good sense must have been common sense in all times; and what we call learning is but the knowledge of the sense of our predecessors. Therefore they who say our thoughts are not our own because they resemble the Ancients may as well say our faces are not our own because they are like our fathers; and, indeed, it is very unreasonable that people should expect us to be scholars and yet be angry to find us so.

I fairly confess that I have served myself all I could by reading; that I made use of the judgment of authors dead and living; that I omitted no means in my power to be informed of my errors, both by my friends and enemies. But the true reason these pieces are not more correct is owing to the consideration how short a time they, and I, have to live. One may be ashamed to consume half one's days in bringing sense and rhyme together; and what critic can be so unreasonable as not to leave a man time enough for any more serious employment or more agreeable amusement?

The only plea I shall use for the favor of the public is that I have as great a respect for it as most authors have for themselves, and that I have sacrificed much of my own self-love for its sake in preventing not only many mean things from seeing the light, but many which I thought tolerable. I would not be like those authors who forgive themselves some particular lines for the sake of a whole poem and vice versa a whole poem for the sake of some particular lines. I believe no one qualification is so likely to make a good writer as the power of rejecting his own thoughts; and it must be this (if anything) that can give me a chance to be one. For what I have published, I can only hope to be pardoned; but for what I have burned, I deserve to be praised. On this account the world is under some obligation to me and owes me the justice in return to look upon no verses as mine that are not inserted in this collection. And perhaps nothing could make it worth my while to own what are really so but to avoid the imputation of so many dull and immoral things as, partly by malice and partly by ignorance, have been ascribed to me. I must farther acquit myself of the presumption of having lent my name to recommend any miscellanies or works of other men, a thing I never thought becoming a person who has hardly credit enough to answer for his own.

In this office of collecting my pieces, I am altogether uncertain whether to look upon myself as a man building a monument or burying the dead.

If time shall make it the former, may these poems (as long as they last) remain as a testimony that their author never made his talents subservient to the mean and unworthy ends of party or self-interest; the gratification of public prejudices or private passions; the flattery of the undeserving or the insult of the unfortunate. If I have written well, let it be considered that 'tis what no man can do without good sense, a quality that not only renders one capable of being a good writer but a good man. And if I have made any acquisition in the opinion of anyone under the notion of the former, let it be continued to me under no other title than that of the latter.

But if this publication be only a more solemn funeral of my remains, I desire it may be known that I die in charity and in my senses, without any murmurs against the justice of this age or any mad appeals to posterity. I declare I shall think the world in the right and quietly submit to every truth which time shall discover to the prejudice of these writings, not so much as wishing so irrational a thing as that everybody should be deceived merely for my credit. However, I desire it may then be considered that there are very few things in this collection which were not written under the age of five and twenty, so that my youth may be made (as it never fails to be in executions) a case of compassion. That I was never so concerned about my works as to vindicate them in print, believing if anything was good it would defend itself and what was bad could never be defended. That I used no artifice to raise or continue a reputation, depreciated no dead author I was obliged to, bribed no living one with unjust praise, insulted no adversary with ill language, or, when I could not attack a rival's works, encouraged reports against his morals. To conclude, if this volume perish, let it serve as a warning to the critics not to take too much pains for the future to destroy such things as will die of themselves, and a *memento mori* to some of my vain contemporaries, the poets, to teach them that when real merit is wanting, it avails nothing to have been encouraged by the great, commended by the eminent, and favored by the public in general.

From Pope's Correspondence

On Wit

To William Wycherley, December 26, 1704

I think with you that whatever lesser wits have risen since his [Dryden's] death are but like stars appearing when the sun is set, that twinkle only in his absence and with the rays they have borrowed from him. Our wit (as you call it) is but reflection or imitation, therefore scarce to be called ours. True wit, I believe, may be defined a justness of thought and a facility of expression, or (in the midwives' phrase) a perfect conception with an easy delivery. However, this is far from a complete definition; pray help me to a better, as I doubt not you can.[1]

To Wycherley, April 10, 1706

I have done all that I thought could be of advantage to them.[2] Some I have contracted, as we do sunbeams, to improve their energy and force; some I have taken quite away, as we take branches from a tree to add to the fruit; others I have entirely new expressed and turned more into poetry. Donne (like one of his successors) had infinitely more wit than he wanted versification; for the great dealers in wit, like those in trade, take least pains to set off their goods, while the haberdashers of small wit spare for no decorations or ornaments. You have commissioned me to paint your shop, and I have done my best to brush you up like your neighbors. But I can no more pretend to the merit of the production than a midwife to the virtues and good qualities of the child she helps into the light.[3]

To Wycherley, November 29, 1707

I must take some notice of what you say of "my pains to make your Dulness methodical" and of your hint that "the

1. *Corr.*, I, 2.
2. Pope is revising and correcting Wycherley's poems.
3. *Corr.*, I, 16.

sprightliness of wit despises method."⁴ This is true enough if
by *wit* you mean no more than *fancy* or *conceit;* but in the
better notion of wit, considered as propriety, surely *method* is
not only necessary for perspicuity and harmony of parts, but
gives beauty even to the minute and particular thoughts, which
receive an additional advantage from those which precede or follow in their due place: according to a simile Mr. Dryden used
in conversation, of feathers in the crowns of the wild Indians,
which they not only choose for the beauty of their colors but
place them in such a manner as to reflect a lustre on each other.
I will not disguise any of my sentiments from you: to methodize,
in your case, is full as necessary as to strike out; otherwise you
had better destroy the whole frame and reduce them into single
thoughts in prose, like Rochefoucauld, as I have more than once
hinted to you.⁵

ON VERSIFICATION

To Henry Cromwell, November 25, 1710

Your mention in this and your last letter of the defect in
numbers of several of our poets puts me upon communicating a
few thoughts, or rather doubts, of mine on that head, some of
which 'tis likely I may have hinted to you formerly in conversation; but I will here put together all the little niceties I can
recollect in the compass of my observation.

1. As to the hiatus, it is certainly to be avoided as often as
possible; but, on the other hand, since the reason of it is only
for the sake of the numbers, so, if to avoid it we incur another
fault against their smoothness, methinks the very end of that
nicety is destroyed. As when we say (for instance) "But th'
old have interest ever in their view" to avoid the hiatus in "The

---

4. Wycherley had commented on Pope's revision of his poem on Dulness:
"And now for the pains you have taken to recommend my *Dulness* by making it more methodical, I give you a thousand thanks; since true and natural
Dulness is shown more by its pretence to form and method, as the sprightliness of wit by its despising both." *Corr.,* I, 33.

5. *Corr.,* I, 34.

old have interest," does not the ear in this place tell us that the hiatus is smoother, less constrained, and so preferable to the caesura?

2. I would except against all expletives in verse, as "do" before verbs plural, or even too frequent use of "did" and "does," to change the termination of the rhyme, all these being against the usual manner of speech and mere fillers up of unnecessary syllables.

3. Monosyllable-lines, unless very artfully managed, are stiff, languishing, and hard.

4. The repeating the same rhymes within four or six lines of each other, which tire the ear with too much of the like sound.

5. The too frequent use of alexandrines, which are never graceful but when there is some majesty added to the verse by them, or when there cannot be found a word in them but what is absolutely needful.

6. Every nice ear must (I believe) have observed that in any smooth English verse of ten syllables there is naturally a pause either at the fourth, fifth, or sixth syllable, as, for example, Waller:

At the fifth: Where'er thy Navy | | spreads her canvas wings.
At the fourth: Homage to thee | | and peace to all she brings.
At the sixth: Like tracks of leverets | | in morning snow.

Now I fancy that to preserve an exact harmony and variety none of these pauses should be continued above three lines together without the interposition of another; else it will be apt to weary the ear with one continued tone; at least it does mine.

7. It is not enough that nothing offends the ear, that the verse be (as the French call it) *coulante;* but a good poet will adapt the very sounds, as well as words, to the things he treats of. So that there is (if one may express it so) a Style of Sound: as in describing a gliding stream the numbers should run easy and flowing, in describing a rough torrent or deluge, sonorous and swelling, and so of the rest. This is evident everywhere in Homer and Virgil, and nowhere else that I know of to any

observable degree. The following examples will make this very plain, which I have taken from Vida:

> *Molle viam tacito lapsu per levia radit.*
> *Incedit tardo molimine subsidendo.*
> *Luctantes ventos, tempestatesque sonoras.*
> *Immenso cum praecipitans ruit oceano nox.*
> *Telum imbelle sine ictu conjecit.*
> *Tolle moras, cape saxa manu, cape robora pastor,*
> *Ferte citi flammas, date tela, repellite pestem.*[6]

This, I think, is what very few observe in practice and is undoubtedly of wonderful force in imprinting the image on the reader. We have one excellent example of this in our language, Mr. Dryden's ode on St. Cecilia's Day entitled "Alexander's Feast, or the Power of Music."[7]

To Cromwell, May 7, 1709

The hiatus, in particular, I would avoid as much as possible, which you are certainly in the right to be a professed enemy to; though I confess I could not think it possible at all times to be avoided by any writer, till I found, by reading the famous French poet Malherbe lately, that there is but one throughout all his poems. I thought your observation true enough to be passed into a rule, but not a rule without exceptions, nor that ever it had been reduced to practice. But this example of one of the correctest and best of their poets has undeceived me, and confirms your opinion very strongly, and much more than Mr.

6. Four of the lines are from Vida's *Art of Poetry;* two are from the *Aeneid:* "Brushes the path in its soft, gentle gliding through the air." Vida, III, 374. "Makes his way by crouching down in ponderous effort." Vida, III, 376. "The struggling winds and the roaring gales." Virgil, I, 53. "As when night rushes headlong over the immense ocean." Vida, III, 425. "Hurled his weak and harmless spear." Virgil, II, 544–545. "Leave off delays, pick up a rock, seize a stick, shepherd; When summoned, bring flames, offer weapons, drive off the pest." Vida, III, 422–423. Translation of Virgil by Fairclough, of Vida by M. A. Brackenridge.

7. *Corr.,* I, 106–108. This letter apparently was later rewritten by Pope and printed as if sent to William Walsh in 1706; see Sherburn's note, *Corr.,* I, 22.

Dryden's authority, who though he made it a rule seldom observed it.[8]

To William Fortescue, October, 1730

I think the gentleman's observations upon the rhythmus[9] every way right and incontestable; and if he extends them in particulars, it cannot but be an useful discourse, to lay down methods to give the last grace and finishing (for so the rhythmus in the sense he uses it may be called) to a poem or oration. But he must give me leave to say this can be done only by examples from Homer, Virgil, Demosthenes, Tully, and a very few more. I have no thoughts of writing upon it, but would practice it wherever I could, which, if performed so as to be seen and felt by the judicious reader, is the same thing; and it ought to be done so distinctly and constantly (had a man time to write correctly) as not to need being pointed out. The author he mentions, Dionysius of Halicarnassus, is much the nicest critic on that subject, I fear rather too minute. I know of none besides those whom he names, except in one chapter of Quintilian and in the book of *Rhetorica ad Herennium*,[10] a few observations. Our English language is certainly more capable of this beauty than the French and Italian; their pauses in the verse are too equal and too near a monotony, ours more various, and I think the better for the consonants, if discreetly managed. Those languages *flow smoothly*, but ours *rolls fully* and freely.[11]

ON CORRECTING, PASTORAL COMEDY, AND BORROWING

To William Walsh, July 2, 1706

I cannot omit the first opportunity of making you my acknowledgements for reviewing those papers[12] of mine. You have no less right to correct me than the same hand that raised a tree has to prune it. I am convinced as well as you that one may cor-

8. *Corr.*, I, 57.
9. An unidentified writer of a treatise on poetic and oratorical rhythm who had sought Pope's advice.
10. An anonymous rhetorical treatise formerly attributed to Cicero.
11. *Corr.*, III, 140.
12. Pope's *Pastorals*.

rect too much; for in poetry, as in painting, a man may lay colors one upon another till they stiffen and deaden the piece. Besides, to bestow heightening on every part is monstrous. Some parts ought to be lower than the rest; and nothing looks more ridiculous than a work where the thoughts, however different in their own nature, seem all on a level. 'Tis like a meadow newly mown, where weeds, grass, and flowers are all laid even and appear undistinguished. I believe, too, that sometimes our first thoughts are the best, as the first squeezing of the grapes makes the finest and richest wine.

I have not attempted anything of pastoral comedy because I think the taste of our age will not relish a poem of that sort.[13] People seek for what they call *wit* on all subjects and in all places, not considering that Nature loves truth so well that it hardly ever admits of flourishing. Conceit is to Nature what paint is to beauty; it is not only needless, but impairs what it would improve. There is a certain majesty in simplicity which is far above all the quaintness of wit, insomuch that the critics have excluded it from the loftiest poetry, as well as the lowest, and forbid it to the epic no less than the pastoral. I should certainly displease all those who are charmed with Guarini and Bonarelli, and imitate Tasso not only in the simplicity of his thoughts but in that of the fable too. If surprising discoveries should have place in the story of a pastoral comedy, I believe it would be more agreeable to probability to make them the effects of chance than of design, intrigue not being very consistent with that innocence which ought to constitute a shepherd's character. There is nothing in all the *Aminta* (as I remember) but happens by mere accident, unless it be the meeting of Aminta with Sylvia at the fountain, which is the contrivance of Daphne, and even that is the most simple in the world. The contrary is observable in *Pastor Fido,* where Corisca is so perfect a mistress of intrigue that the plot could not have been brought to pass without her. I am inclined to think the pastoral comedy has another disad-

13. Walsh had suggested that Pope write a pastoral comedy and had expressed his preference for Tasso's *Aminta* (1573) over Guarini's *Pastor Fido* (1590) and Bonarelli's *Filli di Sciro* (1607).

vantage, as to the manners. Its general design is to make us in
love with the innocence of a rural life, so that to introduce
shepherds of a vicious character must in some measure debase
it; and hence it may come to pass that even the virtuous characters will not shine so much for want of being opposed to their
contraries. These thoughts are purely my own, and therefore I
have reason to doubt them; but I hope your judgment will set
me right.

I would beg your opinion too as to another point: it is how
far the liberty of *borrowing* may extend. I have defended it
sometimes by saying that it seems not so much the perfection
of sense to say things that have *never* been said before as to
express those *best* that have been said *oftenest,* and that writers,
in the case of borrowing from others, are like trees which of
themselves would produce only one sort of fruit but by being
grafted upon others may yield variety. A mutual commerce makes
poetry flourish; but then poets, like merchants, should repay
with something of their own what they take from others, not,
like pirates, make prize of all they meet. I desire you to tell me
sincerely if I have not stretched this license too far in these
pastorals. I hope to become a critic by your precepts and a poet
by your example.[14]

ON CRASHAW

To Cromwell, December 17, 1710

It seems that my late mention of Crashaw, and my quotation
from him, has moved your curiosity. I therefore send you the
whole author, who has held a place among my other books of
this nature for some years, in which time, having read him twice
or thrice, I find him one of those whose works may just deserve
reading. I take this poet to have writ like a gentleman, that is,
at leisure hours, and more to keep out of idleness than to
establish a reputation, so that nothing regular or just can be
expected from him. All that regards design, form, fable (which
is the soul of poetry), all that concerns exactness, or consent
of parts (which is the body), will probably be wanting; only

14. *Corr.,* I, 18–20.

pretty conceptions, fine metaphors, glittering expressions, and something of a neat cast of verse (which are properly the dress, gems, or loose ornaments of poetry) may be found in these verses. This is indeed the case of most other poetical writers of miscellanies; nor can it well be otherwise, since no man can be a true poet who writes for diversion only. These authors should be considered as versifiers and witty men, rather than as poets; and under this head will only fall the thoughts, the expression, and the numbers. These are only the pleasing parts of poetry, which may be judged of at a view and comprehended all at once. And (to express myself like a painter) their coloring entertains the sight, but the lines and life of the picture are not to be inspected too narrowly.

This author formed himself upon Petrarch, or rather upon Marino. His thoughts, one may observe, in the main are pretty, but oftentimes far-fetched and too often strained and stiffened to make them appear the greater. For men are never so apt to think a thing great as when it is odd or wonderful; and inconsiderate authors would rather be admired than understood. This ambition of surprising a reader is the true natural cause of all fustian or bombast in poetry. To confirm what I have said you need but look into his first poem of "The Weeper," where the second, fourth, sixth, fourteenth, twenty-first stanzas are as sublimely dull as the seventh, eighth, ninth, sixteenth, seventeenth, twentieth, and twenty-third stanzas of the same copy are soft and pleasing; and if these last want anything, it is an easier and more unaffected expression. The remaining thoughts in that poem might have been spared, being either but repetitions or very trivial and mean. And by this example in the first one may guess at all the rest to be like this, a mixture of tender gentle thoughts and suitable expressions, of forced and inextricable conceits, and of needless fillers-up to the rest. From all which it is plain this author writ fast and set down what came uppermost. A reader may skim off the froth and use the clear underneath, but if he goes too deep will meet with a mouthful of dregs; either the top or bottom of him are good for little, but what he did in his own, natural, middle way is best.

To speak of his numbers is a little difficult, they are so various and irregular and mostly Pindaric. 'Tis evident his heroic verse (the best example of which is his "Music's Duel") is carelessly made up; but one may imagine from what it now is that, had he taken more care, it had been musical and pleasing enough, not extremely majestic, but sweet. And the time considered of his writing, he was (even as uncorrect as he is) none of the worst versificators.

I will just observe that the best pieces of this author are "A Paraphrase on Psalm 23," "On Lessius," "Epitaph on Mr. Ashton," "Wishes to his (Supposed) Mistress," and the *Dies Irae*.[15]

ON VOLTAIRE'S *La Henriade*

To Viscount Bolingbroke, April 9, 1724

It is but this week that I have been well enough in my head to read the poem of the *League*[16] with the attention it deserves. Next to my obligation to M. de Voltaire for writing it is that I owe to you for sending it. I cannot pretend to judge with any exactness of the beauties of a foreign language which I understand but imperfectly; I can only tell my thoughts in relation to the design and conduct of the poem, or the sentiments. I think the forming the machines upon the allegorical persons of virtues and vices very reasonable, it being equally proper to ancient and modern subjects and to all religions and times; nor do we look upon them so much as heathen divinities as natural passions. This is not the case when Jupiter, Juno, etc., are introduced, who, though sometimes considered as physical powers, yet that sort of allegory lies not open enough to the apprehension. We care not to study or anatomize a poem, but only to read it for our entertainment. It should certainly be a sort of machinery for the meaning of which one is not at a loss for a moment; without something of this nature his poem would too much resemble Lucan or Silius; and indeed, the subject

---

15. *Corr.,* I, 109–111.

16. *La Henriade* was originally published (1723) as *La Ligue;* an heroic poem in ten cantos, it relates the struggle of Henry IV with the Catholic League.

being so modern, a more violent or remote kind of fable or fiction would not suit it. If I have anything to wish on this head, it were to have a little more of the *fictitious* (I dare not say the *wonderful*, for the reason just now given); yet that would give it a greater resemblance to the ancient epic poem. He has helped it much, in my opinion, by throwing so much of the story into narration and entering at once into the middle of the subject, as well as by making the action single, namely only the siege of Paris. This brings it nearer the model of Homer and Virgil; yet I can't help fancying if the fabulous part were a little more extended into descriptions and speeches, etc., it would be of service. And from this very cause methinks that book which treats of the King's love to Madame Gabrielle appears more of a poem than the rest. Discord and Policy[17] might certainly do and say something more, and so I judge of some other occasions for invention and description which methinks are dropped too suddenly.

As to all the parts of the work which relate to the actions or sentiments of men, or to characters and manners, they are undoubtedly excellent and the *fort* of the poem. His characters and sentences are not like Lucan's, too professed or formal and particularized, but full short and judicious, and seem naturally to rise from an occasion either of telling what the man *was* or what he thought. It seems to me that his judgment of mankind and his observation of human actions in a lofty and philosophical view is one of the principal characteristics of the writer, who, however, is not less a poet for being a man of sense (as Seneca and his nephew were). Do not smile when I add that I esteem him for that honest, principled spirit of true religion which shines through the whole, and from whence (unknown as I am to M. de Voltaire) I conclude him at once a free thinker and a lover of quiet; no bigot, but yet no heretic; one who honors authority and national sanctions without prejudice to truth or charity; one who has studied controversy less than reason, and the Fathers less than mankind; in a word, one worthy from his

17. Two of the allegorical characters in the poem.

rational temper of that share of friendship and intimacy with which you honor him.[18]

ON LEVELS OF STYLE

To the Earl of Oxford, March 3, 1725/26

For I am going to tell the world[19] that if they don't keep quite awake over part of my Homer it is because I thought it my duty to observe a certain mediocrity of style, agreeable to conversation and dialogue, which is called the narrative and ought to be low, being put into the mouths of persons not of the highest condition or of a person acting in the disguise of a poor wanderer and speaking in that character of consequence, as Ulysses must in reason be supposed to do or Ulysses was not the wise man we are to take him for. Nothing is so ridiculous as the lofty or poetical style in such parts, which yet many poets (and no very mean ones) are often guilty of, especially in our modern tragedy, where one continued sameness of diction runs through all their characters; and our best actors from hence have got the custom of speaking constantly the most indifferent things in a pompous, elevated voice; 'tis not so properly speaking as vociferating. This goes even to their pronouncing of proper names, those of the Greeks and Romans; they sound as if there were some great energy and mightiness of meaning in the very syllables of "Fabius," "Antony," and "Metellus," etc. In like manner our modern poets preserve a painful equality of fustian throughout their whole epic or tragic works, like travelling all along on the ridge of a hill, which is not half so pleasant as sometimes rising and sometimes descending gently into the vale, as the way leads, and as the end of the journey directs. To write thus upon low subjects is really the true sublime of ridicule, 'tis the sublime of *Don Quixote;* but 'tis strange men should not see it is by no means so of the humbler and narrative parts of poetry. It leaves no distinction between the language of the gods, which is when the muse or the gods speak, and that of men in the conversation and dialogues. Even in set harangues or orations,

18. *Corr.*, II, 228–229.
19. In the Postscript to the *Odyssey*.

this painted, florid style would be ridiculous. Tully and Demosthenes spoke often figuratively, but not poetically, and the very figures of oratory are vastly different from those of poetry; still it is (even in them) much below that language of the gods which I was speaking of.[20]

ON HIS SATIRE

To Dr. Arbuthnot, July 26, 1734

What you recommend to me[21] with the solemnity of a last request shall have its due weight with me. That disdain and indignation against vice is (I thank God) the only disdain and indignation I have. It is sincere, and it will be a lasting one. But sure it is as impossible to have a just abhorrence of vice without hating the vicious as to bear a true love for virtue without loving the good. To reform and not to chastise I am afraid is impossible, and that the best precepts, as well as the best laws, would prove of small use if there were no examples to enforce them. To attack vices in the abstract, without touching persons, may be safe fighting indeed, but it is fighting with shadows. General propositions are obscure, misty, and uncertain, compared with plain, full, and home examples. Precepts only apply to our reason, which in most men is but weak; examples are pictures, and strike the senses, nay raise the passions, and call in those (the strongest and most general of all motives) to the aid of reformation. Every vicious man makes the case his own; and that is the only way by which such men can be affected, much less deterred. So that to chastise is to reform. The only sign by which I found my writings ever did any good, or had any weight, has been that they raised the anger of bad men. And my greatest comfort and encouragement to proceed has been to see that those who have no shame and no fear of anything else have appeared touched by my satires.

20. *Corr.*, II, 370.
21. Arbuthnot had written Pope: "I make it my last request that you continue that noble disdain and abhorrence of vice which you seem naturally endued with, but still with a due regard to your own safety, and study more to reform than chastise, though the one often cannot be effected without the other." *Corr.*, III, 417.

As to your kind concern for my safety, I can guess what occasions it at this time. Some characters I have drawn are such that, if there be any who deserve them, 'tis evidently a service to mankind to point those men out, yet such as, if all the world gave them, none I think will own they take to themselves. But if they should, those of whom all the world think in such a manner must be men I cannot fear. Such in particular as have the meanness to do mischiefs in the dark have seldom the courage to justify them in the face of day; the talents that make a cheat or a whisperer are not the same that qualify a man for an insulter; and, as to private villainy, it is not so safe to join in an assassination as in a libel. I will consult my safety so far as I think becomes a prudent man, but not so far as to omit anything which I think becomes an honest one. As to personal attacks beyond the law, every man is liable to them; as for danger within the law, I am not guilty enough to fear any. For the good opinion of all the world, I know it is not to be had; for that of worthy men, I hope I shall not forfeit it; for that of the great, or those in power, I may wish I had it, but if through misrepresentations (too common about persons in that station) I have it not, I shall be sorry, but not miserable in the want of it.

It is certain much freer satirists than I have enjoyed the encouragement and protection of the princes under whom they lived. Augustus and Mecaenas made Horace their companion, though he had been in arms on the side of Brutus; and allow me to remark it was out of the suffering party, too, that they favored and distinguished Virgil. You will not suspect me of comparing myself with Virgil and Horace, nor even with another court favorite, Boileau. I have always been too modest to imagine my panegyrics were incense worthy of a court; and that, I hope, will be thought the true reason why I have never offered any. I would only have observed that it was under the greatest princes and best ministers that moral satirists were most encouraged, and that then poets exercised the same jursidiction over the follies as historians did over the vices of men. It may also be worth considering whether Augustus himself makes the greater figure in the writings of the former or of the latter. And whether Nero and

Domitian do not appear as ridiculous for their false taste and affectation in Persius and Juvenal as odious for their bad government in Tacitus and Suetonius. In the first of these reigns it was that Horace was protected and caressed, and in the latter that Lucan was put to death and Juvenal banished.[22]

22. *Corr.*, III, 419–420. This letter appears to be an expansion of Pope's actual reply to Arbuthnot (August 2, 1734). Professor Sherburn remarks of the text printed here, "It is most probably a 'forgery,' but it is certainly Pope's best defence in prose of his satire, and as such is invaluable." III, 419n.

Peri Bathous:
Of the Art of Sinking in Poetry (1728)

CHAPTER I

It hath been long (my dear countrymen[1]) the subject of my concern and surprise that whereas numberless poets, critics, and orators have compiled and digested the art of ancient poesy, there hath not arisen among us one person so public spirited as to perform the like for the modern, although it is universally known that our every-way-industrious Moderns, both in the weight of their writings and in the velocity of their judgments, do so infinitely excel the said Ancients.

Nevertheless, too true it is that while a plain and direct road is paved to their ὕψος or *sublime*, no track has been yet chalked out to arrive at our βάθος or *profund*. The Latins, as they came between the Greeks and us, make use of the word *altitudo*, which implies equally height and depth. Wherefore, considering with no small grief how many promising geniuses of this age are wandering (as I may say) in the dark without a guide, I have undertaken this arduous but necessary task to lead them as it were by the hand, and step by step, the gentle downhill way to the Bathos, the bottom, the end, the central point, the *non plus ultra* of true modern poesy!

When I consider (my dear countrymen) the extent, fertility, and populousness of our lowlands of Parnassus, the flourishing state of our trade, and the plenty of our manufacture, there are two reflections which administer great occasion of surprise: the one, that all dignities and honors should be bestowed upon the exceeding few meager inhabitants of the top of the mountain;

---

1. Martinus Scriblerus, though of German extraction, was born in England. *Vid.* his *Life* and *Memoirs,* which will speedily be published [Pope].

the other, that our own nation should have arrived to that pitch
of greatness it now possesses without any regular system of laws.
As to the first, it is with great pleasure I have observed of late the
gradual decay of delicacy and refinement among mankind, who
are become too reasonable to require that we should labor with
infinite pains to come up to the taste of those mountaineers,
when they without any may condescend to ours. But as we have
now an unquestionable majority on our side, I doubt not but
we shall shortly be able to level the Highlanders and procure a
farther vent for our own product, which is already so much
relished, encouraged, and rewarded by the nobility and gentry
of Great Britain.

Therefore, to supply our former defect, I purpose to collect
the scattered rules of our art into regular institutes, from the
example and practice of the deep geniuses of our nation, imitating herein my predecessors, the master of Alexander and the
secretary of the renowned Zenobia.[2] And in this my undertaking
I am the more animated as I expect more success than has
attended even those great critics, since their laws (though they
might be good) have ever been slackly executed, and their precepts (however strict) obeyed only by fits and by a very small
number.

At the same time I intend to do justice upon our neighbors,
inhabitants of the upper Parnassus, who, taking advantage of
the rising ground, are perpetually throwing down rubbish, dirt,
and stones upon us, never suffering us to live in peace. These
men, while they enjoy the crystal stream of Helicon, envy us
our common water, which (thank our stars), though it is somewhat muddy, flows in much greater abundance. Nor is this the
greatest injustice we have to complain of; for though it is evident that we never made the least attempt or inroad into *their*
territories, but lived contented in our native fens, they have
often not only committed petty larcenies upon our borders, but
driven the country and carried off at once *whole cartloads* of
our manufacture, to reclaim some of which stolen goods is part
of the design of this treatise.

2. Aristotle and Longinus.

For we shall see in the course of this work that our greatest adversaries have sometimes descended towards us, and doubtless might now and then have arrived at the Bathos itself, had it not been for that mistaken opinion they all entertained, that the rules of the Ancients were equally necessary to the Moderns, than which there cannot be a more grievous error, as will be amply proved in the following discourse.

And indeed when any of these have gone so far as by the light of their own genius to attempt upon *new* models, it is wonderful to observe how nearly they have approached us in those particular pieces, though in all their others they differed *toto coelo*[3] from us.

CHAPTER II

THAT THE BATHOS OR PROFUND IS THE NATURAL TASTE OF MAN AND IN PARTICULAR OF THE PRESENT AGE

The taste of the Bathos is implanted by Nature itself in the soul of man, 'till perverted by custom or example he is taught, or rather compelled, to relish the Sublime. Accordingly, we see the unprejudiced minds of children delight only in such productions and in such images as our true modern writers set before them. I have observed how fast the general taste is returning to this first simplicity and innocence; and if the intent of all poetry be to divert and instruct, certainly that kind which diverts and instructs the greatest number is to be preferred. Let us look round among the admirers of poetry; we shall find those who have a taste of the Sublime to be very few, but the Profund strikes universally and is adapted to every capacity. 'Tis a fruitless undertaking to write for men of a nice and foppish gusto,[4] whom, after all, it is almost impossible to please; and 'tis still more chimerical to write for posterity, of whose taste we cannot make any judgment and whose applause we can never enjoy. It must be confessed our wiser authors have a present end:

Poets wish either to profit or to please[5]

3. Entirely.   4. Taste.
5. *Et prodesse volunt, et delectare poetae.* Horace, *Ars Poetica*, 333, misquoted. Martinus interprets *prodesse* ("to be useful") as "to make a profit."

Their true design is profit or gain, in order to acquire which 'tis necessary to procure applause by administering pleasure to the reader. From whence it follows demonstrably that their productions must be suited to the present taste; and I cannot but congratulate our age on this peculiar felicity, that though we have made indeed great progress in all other branches of luxury, we are not yet debauched with any high relish in poetry but are in this one taste less *nice* than our ancestors. If an art is to be estimated by its success, I appeal to experience whether there have not been, in proportion to their number, as many starving good poets as bad ones.

Nevertheless, in making gain the principal end of our art, far be it from me to exclude any great geniuses of rank or fortune from diverting themselves this way. They ought to be praised no less than those princes who pass their vacant hours in some ingenious mechanical or manual art; and to such as these it would be ingratitude not to own that our art has been often infinitely indebted.

CHAPTER III
THE NECESSITY OF THE BATHOS, PHYSICALLY CONSIDERED

Farthermore, it were great cruelty and injustice if all such authors as cannot write in the other way were prohibited from writing at all. Against this, I draw an argument from what seems to me an undoubted physical maxim, that poetry is a *natural or morbid secretion from the brain*. As I would not suddenly stop a cold in the head or dry up my neighbor's issue, I would as little hinder him from necessary writing. It may be affirmed with great truth that there is hardly any human creature past childhood but at one time or other has had some poetical evacuation, and no question was much the better for it in his health; so true is the saying, "We are born poets."[6] Therefore is the desire of writing properly termed *pruritus*, the *titillation of the generative faculty of the brain;* and the person is said to *conceive*. Now, such as conceive must *bring forth*. I have known a man thoughtful, melancholy, and raving for divers days,

6. *Nascimur poetae.*

but forthwith grow wonderfully easy, lightsome, and cheerful upon a discharge of the peccant humor in exceeding purulent meter. Nor can I question but abundance of untimely deaths are occasioned by want of this laudable vent of unruly passions, yea, perhaps, in poor wretches (which is very lamentable) for mere want of pen, ink, and paper! From hence it follows that a suppression of the very worst poetry is of dangerous consequence to the State. We find by experience that the same humors which vent themselves in summer in ballads and sonnets are condensed by the winter's cold into pamphlets and speeches for and against the ministry. Nay, I know not but many times a piece of poetry may be the most innocent composition of a minister himself.

It is therefore manifest that Mediocrity ought to be allowed, yea indulged, to the good subjects of England. Nor can I conceive how the world has swallowed the contrary as a maxim upon the single authority of that Horace.[7] Why should the Golden Mean and quintessence of all virtues be deemed so offensive only in this art? Or coolness or Mediocrity be so amiable a quality in a man and so detestable in a poet?

However, far be it from me to compare these writers with those great spirits who are born with a *vivacité de pesanteur,* or (as an English author calls it) an "alacrity of sinking," and who by strength of Nature alone can excel. All I mean is to evince the necessity of rules to these lesser geniuses, as well as the usefulness of them to the greater.

CHAPTER IV
THAT THERE IS AN ART OF THE BATHOS OR PROFUND

We come now to prove that there is an art of sinking in poetry. Is there not an architecture of vaults and cellars as well as of lofty domes and pyramids? Is there not as much skill and labor in making of dikes as in raising of mounts? Is there not an

7. *Mediocribus esse poetis*
   Non dii, non homines, etc. Hor. [Pope]
   Ars Poetica, 372–373, slightly misquoted. "Neither gods nor men allow poets to be mediocre." Martinus deliberately confuses "mediocre" with the "Golden Mean."

art of diving as well as of flying? And will any sober practitioner affirm that a diving engine is not of singular use in making him long-winded, assisting his sight, and furnishing him with other ingenious means of keeping under water?

If we search the authors of antiquity, we shall find as few to have been distinguished in the true Profound as in the true Sublime. And the very same thing (as it appears from Longinus) had been imagined of that, as now of this: namely, that it was entirely the gift of Nature. I grant that to excel in the Bathos a genius is requisite; yet the rules of art must be allowed so far useful as to add weight, or, as I may say, hang on lead, to facilitate and enforce our descent, to guide us to the most advantageous declivities, and habituate our imagination to a depth of thinking. Many there are that can fall, but few can arrive at the felicity of falling gracefully; much more for a man who is amongst the lowest of the creation at the very bottom of the atmosphere, to descend beneath himself is not so easy a task, unless he calls in art to his assistance. It is with the Bathos as with small beer, which is indeed vapid and insipid if left at large and let abroad; but, being by our rules confined and well stopped, nothing grows so frothy, pert, and bouncing.

The Sublime of Nature is the sky, the sun, moon, stars, etc. The Profound of Nature is gold, pearls, precious stones, and the treasures of the deep, which are inestimable as unknown. But all that lies between these, as corn, flowers, fruits, animals, and things for the mere use of man are of mean price and so common as not to be greatly esteemed by the curious, it being certain that anything of which we know the true use cannot be invaluable: which affords a solution why common sense hath either been totally despised or held in small repute by the greatest modern critics and authors.

CHAPTER V

OF THE TRUE GENIUS FOR THE PROFOUND
AND BY WHAT IT IS CONSTITUTED

And I will venture to lay it down as the first maxim and cornerstone of this our art, that whoever would excel therein must studiously avoid, detest, and turn his head from all the ideas, ways, and workings of that pestilent foe to wit and destroyer of fine figures which is known by the name of *common sense*. His business must be to contract the true *goût de travers*[8] and to acquire a most happy, uncommon, unaccountable way of thinking.

He is to consider himself as a grotesque painter, whose works would be spoiled by an imitation of Nature or uniformity of design. He is to mingle bits of the most various or discordant kinds—landscape, history, portraits, animals—and connect them with a great deal of flourishing by heads or tails, as it shall please his imagination and contribute to his principal end, which is to glare by strong oppositions of colors and surprise by contrariety of images. "Serpents are paired with birds, and lambs with tigers."[9]

His design ought to be like a labyrinth, out of which nobody can get you clear but himself. And since the great art of all poetry is to mix truth and fiction in order to join the credible with the surprising, our author shall produce the credible by painting Nature in her lowest simplicity and the surprising by contradicting common opinion. In the very manners he will affect the marvellous; he will draw Achilles with the patience of Job, a prince talking like a Jack-pudding, a maid of honor selling bargains,[10] a footman speaking like a philosopher, and a fine gentleman like a scholar. Whoever is conversant in modern plays may make a most noble collection of this kind and, at the same time, form a complete body of modern ethics and morality.

Nothing seemed more plain to our great authors than that the world had long been weary of natural things. How much the contrary is formed to please is evident from the universal applause daily given to the admirable entertainments of harlequins and magicians on our stage. When an audience behold a coach turned into a wheelbarrow, a conjurer into an old woman, or a man's head where his heels should be, how are they struck

8. Taste gone askew.
9. *Serpentes avibus geminentur, tigribus agni.* Horace, *Ars Poetica*, 13.
10. A type of vulgar joke.

with transport and delight? Which can only be imputed to this cause, that each object is changed into that which hath been suggested to them by their own low ideas before.

He ought therefore to render himself master of this happy and antinatural way of thinking to such a degree as to be able, on the appearance of any object, to furnish his imagination with ideas infinitely below it. And his eyes should be like unto the wrong end of a perspective glass, by which all the objects of Nature are lessened.

For example, when a true genius looks upon the sky, he immediately catches the idea of a piece of blue lutestring or a child's mantle.

> The skies, whose spreading volumes scarce have room,
> Spun thin, and wove in Nature's finest Loom,
> The new-born world in their soft lap embraced,
> And all around their starry mantle cast.[11]

If he looks upon a tempest, he shall have the image of a tumbled bed, and describe a succeeding calm in this manner:

> The ocean joyed to see the tempest fled,
> New lays his waves and smoothes his ruffled bed.[12]

The triumphs and acclamations of the angels at the creation of the universe present to his imagination the rejoicings of the Lord Mayor's Day; and he beholds those glorious beings celebrating the Creator by huzzaing, making illuminations, and flinging squibs, crackers, and sky-rockets.

> Glorious illuminations, made on high
> By all the stars and planets of the sky,
> In just degrees and shining order placed,
> Spectators charmed and the blest dwelling graced.
> Thro' all the enlightened air swift fireworks flew,
> Which with repeated shouts glad cherubs threw.

11. *Prince Arthur,* pp. 41–42 [Pope]. The poet is Sir Richard Blackmore. In the notes by Pope which follow, his abbreviations will be expanded.

12. P. 14. N.B. In order to do justice to these great poets, our citations are taken from the best, the last, and most correct editions of their works. That which we use of *Prince Arthur* is in duodecimo, 1714, the fourth edition, revised [Pope].

Comets ascended with their sweeping train,
Then fell in starry showers and glittering rain.
In air ten thousand meteors blazing hung,
Which from th'eternal battlements were flung.[13]

If a man who is violently fond of wit will sacrifice to that passion his friend or his God, would it not be a shame if he who is smit with the love of the Bathos should not sacrifice to it all other transitory regards? You shall hear a zealous protestant deacon invoke a Saint and modestly beseech her only to change the course of providence and destiny for the sake of three or four weighty lines.

Look down, blest Saint, with pity then look down,
Shed on this land thy kinder influence,
And guide us through the mists of Providence,
In which we stray.[14]

Neither will he, if a goodly simile come in his way, scruple to affirm himself an eye-witness of things never yet beheld by man, or never in existence, as thus:

Thus have I seen, in Araby the blest,
A Phoenix couched upon her fun'ral nest.[15]

But to convince you that nothing is so great which a marvelous genius, prompted by this laudable zeal, is not able to lessen, hear how the most sublime of all beings is represented in the following images.

First he is a PAINTER.

Sometimes the Lord of Nature in the air,
Spreads forth his clouds, his sable canvas, where
His pencil, dipped in heavenly color bright,
Paints his fair rainbow, charming to the sight.[16]

Now he is a CHEMIST.

Th' Almighty Chemist does his work prepare,
Pours down his waters on the thirsty plain,

13. P. 50 [Pope].
14. Ambrose Philips on the death of Queen Mary [Pope].
15. Anonymous [Pope].
16. Blackmore, *Job, opt. edit.*, duodecimo, 1716, p. 172 [Pope].

Digests his lightning and distils his rain.[17]

Now he is a WRESTLER.

> Me in his gripping arms th' Eternal took,
> And with such mighty force my body shook,
> That the strong grasp my members sorely bruised,
> Broke all my bones, and all my sinews loosed.[18]

Now a RECRUITING OFFICER.

> For clouds the sun-beams levy fresh supplies,
> And raise recruits of vapors, which arise,
> Drawn from the seas, to muster in the skies.[19]

Now a peaceable GUARANTEE.

> In leagues of peace the neighbors did agree,
> And to maintain them, God was guarantee.[20]

Then he is an ATTORNEY.

> Job, as a vile offender, God indicts,
> And terrible decrees against me writes.
> God will not be my advocate,
> My cause to manage or debate.[21]

In the following lines he is a GOLDBEATER.

> Who the rich metal beats, and then, with care,
> Unfolds the golden leaves, to gild the fields of air.[22]

Then a FULLER.

> ... th' exhaling reeks that secret rise,
> Borne on rebounding sun-beams through the skies,
> Are thickened, wrought, and whitened, till they grow
> A heavenly fleece.[23]

---

17. Blackmore, *Psalm 104*, p. 263 [Pope]. Whenever Pope cites a Biblical paraphrase by Blackmore, his reference is to the volume listed in note 16, above.
18. P. 75 [Pope].
19. P. 170 [Pope].
20. P. 70 [Pope].
21. P. 61 [Pope].
22. P. 181 [Pope].
23. P. 18 [Pope].

A MERCER or PACKER.

> Didst thou one end of air's wide curtain hold,
> And help the bales of ether to unfold;
> Say, which cerulean pile was by thy hand unrolled?[24]

A BUTLER.

> He measures all the drops with wondrous skill,
> Which the black clouds, his floating bottles, fill.[25]

And a BAKER.

> God in the wilderness his table spread,
> And in his airy ovens baked their bread.[26]

CHAPTER VI

OF THE SEVERAL KINDS OF GENIUSES IN THE PROFUND, AND THE MARKS AND CHARACTERS OF EACH

I doubt not but the reader, by this cloud of examples, begins to be convinced of the truth of our assertion that the Bathos is an art, and that the genius of no mortal whatever, following the mere ideas of Nature and unassisted with an habitual, nay laborious peculiarity of thinking, could arrive at images so wonderfully low and unaccountable. The great author from whose treasury we have drawn all these instances (the Father of the Bathos and indeed the Homer of it) has, like that immortal Greek, confined his labors to the greater poetry and thereby left room for others to acquire a due share of praise in inferior kinds. Many painters who could never hit a nose or an eye have with felicity copied a small-pox or been admirable at a toad or a red-herring. And seldom are we without geniuses for still life, which they can work up and stiffen with incredible accuracy.

An universal genius rises not in an age; but when he rises, armies rise in him! He pours forth five or six epic poems with greater facility than five or six pages can be produced by an elaborate and servile copier after Nature or the Ancients. It is

24. P. 174 [Pope].
25. P. 131 [Pope].
26. Blackmore, *Song of Moses*, p. 218 [Pope].

affirmed by Quintilian that the same genius which made Germanicus so great a general would with equal application have made him an excellent heroic poet. In like manner, reasoning from the affinity there appears between arts and sciences, I doubt not but an active catcher of butterflies, a careful and fanciful pattern-drawer, an industrious collector of shells, a laborious and tuneful bagpiper, or a diligent breeder of tame rabbits might severally excel in their respective parts of the Bathos.

I shall range these confined and less copious geniuses under proper classes and (the better to give their pictures to the reader) under the names of animals of some sort or other, whereby he will be enabled, at the first sight of such as shall daily come forth, to know to what kind to refer and with what authors to compare them.

1. The *Flying Fishes:* these are writers who now and then rise upon their fins and fly out of the Profund; but their wings are soon dry, and they drop down to the bottom. G. S.   A. H.   C. G.[27]

2. The *Swallows* are authors that are eternally skimming and fluttering up and down, but all their agility is employed to catch flies. L.T.   W. P.   Lord R.

3. The *Ostriches* are such whose heaviness rarely permits them to raise themselves from the ground; their wings are of no use to lift them up, and their motion is between flying and walking; but then they run very fast. D. F.   L. E.   The Hon. E. H.

4. The *Parrots* are they that repeat another's words in such a hoarse, odd voice that makes them seem their own. W. B.   W. H.   C. C.   The Reverend D. D.

27. Although Pope denied that the initials in this chapter were to be applied to particular writers, their use provoked a violent response from his enemies. Among the writers almost certainly alluded to are Aaron Hill, Charles Gildon, Lewis Theobald, Daniel Defoe, Laurence Eusden, William Broome, Colley Cibber, Leonard Welsted, John Dennis, John Oldmixon, Thomas D'Urfey, General Codrington, and Ambrose Philips. See *Works,* ed. Elwin and Courthope, X, 361–362, and the discussion by Steeves in her edition of *Peri Bathous.*

5. The *Didappers* are authors that keep themselves long out of sight, under water, and come up now and then where you least expected them. L. W.—D. Esq.   The Hon. Sir W. Y.

6. The *Porpoises* are unwieldy and big; they put all their numbers into a great turmoil and tempest, but whenever they appear in plain light (which is seldom) they are only shapeless and ugly monsters. I. D.   C. G.   I. O.

7. The *Frogs* are such as can neither walk nor fly, but can leap and bound to admiration. They live generally in the bottom of a ditch and make a great noise whenever they thrust their heads above water. E. W. I. M. Esq.   T. D.   Gent.

8. The *Eels* are obscure authors that wrap themselves up in their own mud, but are mighty nimble and pert. L. W.   L. T. P. M.   General C.

9. The *Tortoises* are slow and chill, and, like pastoral writers, delight much in gardens. They have for the most part a fine embroidered shell, and underneath it a *heavy lump*. A. P.   W. B. L. E.   The Rt. Hon. E. of S.

These are the chief characteristics of the Bathos, and in each of these kinds we have the comfort to be blessed with sundry and manifold choice spirits in this our island.

CHAPTER VII
OF THE PROFUND, WHEN IT CONSISTS IN THE THOUGHT

We have already laid down the principles upon which our author is to proceed and the manner of forming his thoughts by familiarizing his mind to the lowest objects, to which it may be added that vulgar conversation will greatly contribute. There is no question but the garret or the printer's boy may often be discerned in the compositions made in such scenes and company; and much of Mr. Curll himself has been insensibly infused into the works of his learned writers.

The physician, by the study and inspection of urine and ordure, approves himself in the sciences; and in like sort should our author accustom and exercise his imagination upon the dregs of Nature.

This will render his thoughts truly and fundamentally low

and carry him many fathoms beyond mediocrity. For, certain it
is (though some lukewarm heads imagine they may be safe by
temporizing between the extremes) that where there is [not] a
triticalness[28] or mediocrity in the *thought*, it can never be sunk
into the genuine and perfect Bathos by the most elaborate low
expression. It can, at most, be only carefully obscured or meta-
phorically debased. But 'tis the thought alone that strikes and
gives the whole that spirit which we admire and stare at. For
instance, in that ingenious piece on a lady's drinking the Bath-
waters:

> She drinks! She drinks! Behold the matchless Dame!
> To her 'tis water, but to us 'tis flame:
> Thus fire is water, water fire, by turns,
> And the same stream at once both cools and burns.[29]

What can be more easy and unaffected than the *diction* of these
verses? 'Tis the turn of *thought* alone and the variety of imagination that charm and surprise us. And when the same lady goes
into the bath, the thought (as in justness it ought) goes still
deeper:

> Venus beheld her, 'midst her crowd of slaves,
> And thought herself just risen from the waves.[30]

How much out of the way of common sense is this reflection of
Venus, not knowing herself from the Lady?

Of the same nature is that noble mistake of a frighted stag in
full chase, of which the poet:

> Hears his own feet, and thinks they sound like more;
> And fears the hind feet will o'ertake the fore.

So astonishing as these are, they yield to the following, which
is profundity itself:

> None but himself can be his parallel.[31]

28. *Not:* omitted in the first edition; *triticalness:* triteness.
29. Anonymous [Pope].
30. *Idem.* [Pope].
31. Theobald, *Double Distress* [Pope]. Pope means *Double Falsehood, or
the Distrest Lovers.*

unless it may seem borrowed from the thought of that master
of a show in Smithfield who writ in large letters, over the picture
of his elephant, "This is the greatest elephant in the world,
except himself."

However, our next instance is certainly an original. Speaking
of a beautiful infant:

> So fair thou art, that if great Cupid be
> A child, as poets say, sure thou art he.
> Fair Venus would mistake thee for her own,
> Did not thy eyes proclaim thee not her son.
> There all the lightnings of thy mother's shine,
> And with a fatal brightness kill in thine.

First he is Cupid, then he is not Cupid; first Venus would mistake
him, then she would not mistake him; next his eyes are his
mother's; and lastly they are not his mother's but his own.

Another author, describing a poet that shines forth amidst
a circle of critics:

> Thus Phoebus through the Zodiac takes his way,
> And amid monsters rises into day.[32]

What a peculiarity is here of invention? The author's pencil, like
the wand of Circe, turns all into monsters at a stroke. A great
genius takes things in the lump, without stopping at minute
considerations. In vain might the Ram, the Bull, the Goat, the
Lion, the Crab, the Scorpion, the Fishes all stand in his way as
mere natural animals; much more might it be pleaded that a
pair of scales, an old man, and two innocent children were no
monsters. There were only the Centaur and the Maid that could
be esteemed out of Nature. But what of that? With a boldness
peculiar to these daring geniuses, what he found not monsters,
he made so.

32. From William Broome's "Epistle to my Friend Mr. Elijah Fenton"
(Elwin and Courthope).

CHAPTER VIII
OF THE PROFUND CONSISTING IN THE CIRCUMSTANCES,
AND OF AMPLIFICATION AND PERIPHRASE IN GENERAL

What in a great measure distinguishes other writers from ours is their choosing and separating such circumstances in a description as illustrate or elevate the subject.

The circumstances which are most natural are obvious, therefore not astonishing or peculiar. But those that are far-fetched or unexpected or hardly compatible will surprise prodigiously. These therefore we must principally hunt out; but above all preserve a laudable prolixity, presenting the whole and every side at once of the image to view. For choice and distinction are not only a curb to the spirit and limit the descriptive faculty, but also lessen the book, which is frequently of the worst consequence of all to our author.

When Job says in short, "He washed his feet in butter," (a circumstance some poets would have softened or passed over), hear how it is spread out by the Great Genius:

> With teats distended with their milky store,
> Such num'rous lowing herds, before my door,
> Their painful burden to unload did meet,
> That we with butter might have washed our feet.[33]

How cautious! and particular! He had (says our author) so many herds, which herds thrived so well, and thriving so well, gave so much milk, and that milk produced so much butter, that if he *did not*, he *might* have washed his feet in it.

The ensuing description of Hell is no less remarkable in the circumstances:

> In flaming heaps the raging ocean rolls,
> Whose livid waves involve despairing souls;
> The liquid burnings dreadful colors show,
> Some deeply red, and others faintly blue.[34]

Could the most minute Dutch painter have been more exact? How inimitably circumstantial is this also of a war-horse!

33. Blackmore, *Job*, p. 133 [Pope].
34. *Prince Arthur*, p. 89 [Pope].

His eye-balls burn, he wounds the smoking plain,
And knots of scarlet ribbon deck his mane.[35]

Of certain cudgel-players:

They brandish high in air their threat'ning staves,
Their hands a woven guard of ozier saves,
In which they fix their hazel weapon's end.[36]

Who would not think the poet had passed his whole life at
wakes in such laudable diversions? He even teaches us how to
hold and to make a cudgel!

Periphrase is another great aid to prolixity, being a diffused
circumlocutory manner of expressing a known idea, which should
be so mysteriously couched as to give the reader the pleasure
of guessing what it is that the author can possibly mean, and a
surprise when he finds it.

The poet I last mentioned is incomparable in this figure:

A waving sea of heads was round me spread,
And still fresh streams the gazing deluge fed.[37]

Here is a waving sea of heads, which by a fresh stream of heads
grows to be a gazing deluge of heads. You come at last to find
it means a "great crowd."

How pretty and how genteel is the following:

Nature's confectioner,
Whose suckets are moist alchemy:
The still of his refining mold,
Minting the garden into gold.[38]

What is this but a bee gathering honey?

Little Siren of the stage,
Empty warbler, breathing lyre,
Wanton gale of fond desire,
Tuneful mischief, vocal spell.[39]

35. Anonymous [Pope].
36. *Prince Arthur*, p. 197 [Pope].
37. *Job*, p. 78 [Pope].
38. Cleveland [Pope].
39. Philips to C—— [Pope]; i.e., Ambrose Philips, "To Signora Cuzzoni."

Who would think this was only a poor gentlewoman that sung finely?

We may define *Amplification* to be making the most of a thought; it is the spinning wheel of the Bathos, which draws out and spreads it in the finest thread. There are Amplifiers who can extend half a dozen thin thoughts over a whole folio, but for which the tale of many a vast romance and the substance of many a fair volume might be reduced into the size of a primer.

In the *Book of Job* are these words, "Hast thou commanded the morning, and caused the dayspring to know his place?" How is this extended by the most celebrated Amplifier of our age?

> Canst thou set forth th' etherial mines on high,
> Which the refulgent ore of light supply?
> Is the celestial furnace to thee known,
> In which I melt the golden metal down?
> Treasures, from whence I deal out light as fast,
> As all my stars and lavish suns can waste.[40]

The same author hath amplified a passage in the 104th Psalm: "He looks on the earth, and it trembles. He touches the hills, and they smoke."

> The hills forget they're fixed, and in their fright,
> Cast off their weight, and ease themselves for flight:
> The woods, with terror winged, out-fly the wind,
> And leave the heavy, panting hills behind.[41]

You here see the hills not only trembling, but shaking off their woods from their backs, to run the faster. After this you are presented with a foot race of mountains and woods, where the woods distance the mountains, that, like corpulent pursy fellows, come puffing and panting a vast way behind them.

CHAPTER IX
OF IMITATION, AND THE MANNER OF IMITATING

That the true authors of the Profund are to imitate diligently the examples in their own way is not to be questioned, and that

40. *Job*, p. 180 [Pope].
41. P. 267 [Pope].

divers have by this means attained to a depth whereunto their
own weight could not have carried them is evident by sundry
instances. Who sees not that De F—— was the poetical son of
Withers, T—te of Ogilby, E. W—rd of John Taylor, and E—n
of Bl—k—re? Therefore, when we sit down to write, let us bring
some great author to our mind and ask ourselves this question:
how would Sir Richard have said this? Do I express myself as
simply as A. Ph——? or flow my numbers with the quiet thought-
lessness of Mr. W—st—d?[42]

But it may seem somewhat strange to assert that our pro-
ficient should also read the works of those famous poets who
have excelled in the Sublime; yet is not this a paradox. As Virgil
is said to have read Ennius, out of his dunghill to draw gold,
so may our author read Shakespeare, Milton, and Dryden for
the contrary end, to bury their gold in his own dunghill. A true
genius, when he finds anything lofty or shining in them, will
have the skill to bring it down, take off the gloss, or quite discharge the color by some ingenious circumstance or periphrase,
some addition or diminution, or by some of those figures the
use of which we shall show in our next chapter.

The Book of Job is acknowledged to be infinitely sublime, and
yet has not our Father of the Bathos reduced it in every page?
Is there a passage in all Virgil more painted up and labored
than the description of Aetna in the third *Aeneid?*

> *Horrificis juxta tonat Aetna ruinis,*
> *Interdumque atram prorumpit ad aethera nubem,*
> *Turbine fumantem piceo, et candente favilla,*
> *Attollitque globos flammarum, et sidera lambit.*
> *Interdum scopulos avulsaque viscera montis*
> *Erigit eructans, liquefactaque saxa sub auras*
> *Cum gemitu glomerat, fundoque exaestuat imo.*

(I beg pardon of the gentle English reader and such of our writers
as understand not Latin.) But lo! how this is taken down by our
British poet, by the single happy thought of throwing the mountain into a fit of the *colic:*

42. The references are to Defoe, Tate, Edward Ward, Eusden, Blackmore,
Ambrose Philips, and Welsted.

> Aetna, and all the burning mountains, find
> Their kindled stores with inbred storms of wind
> Blown up to rage, and, roaring out, complain,
> As torn with inward gripes and torturing pain:
> Lab'ring, they cast their dreadful vomit round,
> And with their melted bowels spread the ground.[43]

Horace, in search of the Sublime, struck his head against the stars;[44] but Empedocles, to fathom the Profund, threw himself into Aetna. And who but would imagine our excellent modern had also been there, from this description?

Imitation is of two sorts: the first is when we force to our own purposes the thoughts of others; the second consists in copying the imperfections or blemishes of celebrated authors. I have seen a play professedly writ in the style of Shakespeare, wherein the greatest resemblance lay in one single line: "And so good morrow t' ye, good master Lieutenant."[45] And sundry poems in imitation of Milton, where with the utmost exactness and not so much as one exception, *nevertheless* was constantly *nathless; embroidered* was *broidered; hermits* were *eremites; disdained* was *'sdeigned; shady, umbrageous; enterprise, emprize; pagan, paynim; pinious, pennons; sweet, dulcet; orchards, orchats; bridgework, pontifical;* nay, *her* was *hir,* and *their* was *thir* through the whole poem. And in very deed there is no other way by which the true modern poet could read to any purpose the works of such men as Milton and Shakespeare.

It may be expected that, like other critics, I should next speak of the passions. But as the main end and principal effect of the Bathos is to produce tranquillity of mind (and sure it is a better design to promote sleep than madness), we have little to say on

---

43. *Prince Arthur,* p. 75 [Pope]. The passage from the *Aeneid* (III, 571–577) is more literally translated by Fairclough: "Aetna thunders with terrifying crashes, and now hurls forth to the sky a black cloud, smoking with pitch-black eddy and glowing ashes, and uplifts balls of flame, and licks the stars—now violently vomits forth rocks, the mountain's uptorn entrails, and whirls molten stone skyward with a roar, and boils up from its lowest depths."

44. *Sublimi feriam sidera vertice* [Pope]. "I shall touch the stars with my exalted head." Horace, *Odes,* Bk I, Ode i, 1. 36.

45. From Nicholas Rowe's *Lady Jane Grey,* Act V, scene i (Elwin and Courthope).

this subject. Nor will the short bounds of this discourse allow us to treat at large of the emollients and opiates of poesy, of the cool and the manner of producing it, or of the methods used by our authors in managing the passions. I shall but transiently remark that nothing contributes so much to the cool as the use of wit in expressing passion. The true genius rarely fails of points, conceits, and proper similes on such occasions. This we may term the *pathetic epigrammatical,* in which even puns are made use of with good success. Hereby our best authors have avoided throwing themselves or their readers into any indecent transports.

But forasmuch as it is sometimes needful to excite the passions of our antagonist in the polemic way, the true students in the Low have constantly taken their methods from low life, where they observed that to move anger, use is made of scolding and railing; to move love, of bawdry; to beget favor and friendship, of gross flattery; and to produce fear, by calumniating an adversary with crimes obnoxious to the state. As for shame, it is a silly passion, of which as our authors are incapable themselves, so they would not produce it in others.

Chapter X
Of Tropes and Figures: and First of the Variegating, Confusing, and Reversing Figures

But we proceed to the figures. We cannot too earnestly recommend to our authors the study of the Abuse of Speech. They ought to lay it down as a principle to say nothing in the usual way, but (if possible) in the direct contrary. Therefore the figures must be so turned as to manifest that intricate and wonderful cast of head which distinguishes all writers of this genius, or (as I may say) to refer exactly the mold in which they were formed in all its inequalities, cavities, obliquities, odd crannies, and distortions.

It would be endless, nay impossible, to enumerate all such figures; but we shall content ourselves to range the principal which most powerfully contribute to the Bathos, under three classes.

I. The Variegating, Confusing, or Reversing tropes and figures.

II. The Magnifying, and

III. The Diminishing.

We cannot avoid giving to these the Greek or Roman names; but in tenderness to our countrymen and fellow writers, many of whom, however exquisite, are wholly ignorant of those languages, we have also explained them in our mother tongue.

Of the first sort, nothing so much conduces to the Abuse of Speech as the

CATACHRESIS.

A master of this will say,

> Mow the beard,
> Shave the grass,
> Pin the plank,
> Nail my sleeve.

From whence results the same kind of pleasure to the mind as doth to the eye when we behold Harlequin trimming himself with a hatchet, hewing down a tree with a razor, making his tea in a cauldron, and brewing his ale in a tea-pot, to the incredible satisfaction of the British spectator.

Another source of the Bathos is

THE METONYMY,

the inversion of causes for effects, of inventors for inventions, etc.

> Lac'd in her *cosins* new appeared the bride,
> A *bubble-boy* and *tompion* at her side,
> And with an air divine her *colmar* ply'd.
> And oh! she cries, what slaves I round me see!
> Here a bright Redcoat, there a smart *toupee*.[46]

THE SYNECHDOCHE

which consists in the use of a part for the whole; you may call a young woman sometimes pretty-face and pigs-eyes, and sometimes snotty-nose and draggle-tail. Or of accidents for persons, as a lawyer is called split-cause, a tailor prick-louse, etc. Or of things belonging to a man for the man himself, as a sword-man,

46. "Stays," "tweezer case," "watch," "fan," and a sort of periwig: all words in use in this present year 1727 [Pope].

a gown-man, a T—m T—d—man, a white-staff,[47] a turn-key, etc.

THE APOSIOPESIS

An excellent figure for the ignorant, as "What shall I say?" when one has nothing to say; or "I can no more" when one really can no more, expressions which the gentle reader is so good as never to take in earnest.

THE METAPHOR

The first rule is to draw it from the lowest things, which is a certain way to sink the highest; as when you speak of the thunder of Heaven, say, "The lords above are angry and talk big."[48]

If you would describe a rich man refunding his treasures, express it thus:

> Though he (as said) may riches gorge, the spoil
> Painful in massy vomit shall recoil.
> Soon shall he perish with a swift decay,
> Like his own ordure, cast with scorn away.[49]

The second, that whenever you *start* a metaphor, you must be sure to *run it down* and pursue it as far as it can go. If you get the scent of a state negotiation, follow it in this manner.

> The stones and all the elements with thee
> Shall ratify a strict confederacy;
> Wild beasts their savage temper shall forget,
> And for a firm alliance with thee treat;
> The finny tyrant of the spacious seas
> Shall send a scaly embassy for peace:
> His plighted faith the crocodile shall keep,
> And seeing thee, for joy sincerely weep.[50]

Or if you represent the Creator denouncing war against the wicked, be sure not to omit one circumstance usual in proclaiming and levying war.

47. *T—m T—d—man:* a man who empties cesspools at night; *white-staff:* the Lord Treasurer or other high official.
48. Lee, *Alexander* [Pope]; i.e., Nathaniel Lee, *The Rival Queens, or the Death of Alexander the Great.*
49. Blackmore, *Job,* pp. 91, 93 [Pope].
50. *Job,* p. 22 [Pope].

Envoys and agents, who by my command
Reside in Palestina's land,
To whom commissions I have given,
To manage there the interests of Heaven;
Ye holy heralds who proclaim
Or war or peace, in mine your master's name;
Ye pioneers of Heaven, prepare a road,
Make it plain, direct, and broad;
For I in person will my people head;
For the divine deliverer
Will on his march in majesty appear,
And needs the aid of no confederate pow'r.[51]

Under the article of the Confusing, we rank
THE MIXTURE OF FIGURES,
which raises so many images as to give you no image at all. But
its principal beauty is when it gives an idea just opposite to
what it seemed meant to describe. Thus an ingenious artist painting the spring talks of a "snow" of blossoms and thereby raises
an unexpected picture of winter. Of this sort is the following:

The gaping clouds pour lakes of sulphur down,
Whose livid flashes sick'ning sunbeams drown.[52]

What a noble confusion! Clouds, lakes, brimstone, flames, sunbeams, gaping, pouring, sickening, drowning! All in two lines.
THE JARGON

Thy head shall rise, though buried in the dust,
And midst the clouds his glittering turrets thrust.[53]

Quaere, what are the glittering turrets of a man's head?

Upon the shore, as frequent as the sand,
To meet the prince, the glad Dimetians stand.[54]

Quaere, where these Dimetians stood? and of what size they
were?

Destruction's Empire shall no longer last,

51. Blackmore, Isaiah, Chapter 40 [Pope].
52. Prince Arthur, p. 73 [Pope].
53. Job, p. 107 [Pope].
54. Prince Arthur, p. 157 [Pope].

And Desolation lie for ever waste.[55]

But for Variegation and Confusion of objects, nothing is more useful than

THE ANTITHESIS OR SEE-SAW

whereby contraries and oppositions are balanced in such a way as to cause a reader to remain suspended between them, to his exceeding delight and recreation. Such are these, on a lady who made herself appear out of size by hiding a young princess under her clothes:

> While the kind nymph changing her faultless shape
> Becomes unhandsome, handsomely to 'scape.[56]

On the maids of honor in mourning:

> Sadly they charm, and dismally they please.[57]

> His eyes so bright
> Let in the object; and let out the light.[58]

> The Gods look pale to see us look so red.[59]

> The fairies and their Queen

> In mantles blue came tripping o'er the green.[60]

> All nature felt a reverential shock,
> The sea stood still to see the mountains rock.[61]

CHAPTER XI

THE FIGURES CONTINUED:

OF THE MAGNIFYING AND DIMINISHING FIGURES

A genuine writer of the profund will take care never to *magnify* any object without *clouding* it at the same time; his thought will appear in a true mist and very unlike what it is in Nature. It must always be remembered that darkness is an

55. *Job*, p. 89 [Pope].
56. Waller [Pope].
57. Steele on Queen Mary [Pope].
58. Quarles [Pope].
59. Lee, *Alexander* [Pope].
60. Philips, *Pastorals* [Pope].
61. Blackmore, *Job*, p. 176 [Pope].

essential quality of the Profund, or if there chance to be a glimmering, it must be as Milton expresses it, "No light, but rather darkness visible." The chief figure of this sort is

THE HYPERBOLE OR IMPOSSIBLE

For instance, of a lion:

> He roared so loud, and looked so wondrous grim,
> His very shadow durst not follow him.[62]

Of a lady at dinner:

> The silver whiteness that adorns thy neck,
> Sullies the plate, and makes the napkin black.

Of the same:

> The obscureness of her birth
> Cannot eclipse the lustre of her eyes,
> Which make her all one light.[63]

Of a bull-baiting:

> Up to the stars the sprawling mastives fly,
> And add new monsters to the frighted sky.[64]

Of a scene of misery:

> Behold a scene of misery and woe!
> Here Argus soon might weep himself quite blind,
> Ev'n though he had Briareus' hundred hands
> To wipe those hundred eyes.[65]

And that modest request of two absent lovers:

> Ye gods! annihilate but space and time,
> And make two lovers happy.

The *periphrasis,* which the moderns call the *circumbendibus,* whereof we have given examples in the ninth chapter and shall again in the twelfth.

---

62. *Vetus autor* [Pope].
63. Theobald, *Double Distress* [Pope]; i.e., *Double Falsehood.*
64. Blackmore [Pope].
65. Anonymous [Pope].

To the same class of the Magnifying may be referred the following, which are so excellently modern that we have yet no name for them. In describing a country prospect:

> I'd call them mountains, but can't call them so,
> For fear to wrong them with a name too low;
> While the fair vales beneath so humbly lie,
> That even humble seems a term too high.[66]

III. The third class remains, of the Diminishing figures: and first, the *anticlimax,* where the second line drops quite short of the first, than which nothing creates greater surprise.

On the extent of the British arms:

> Under the tropics is our language spoke,
> And part of Flanders hath received our yoke.[67]

On a warrior:

> And thou Dalhoussy the Great God of War,
> Lieutenant Colonel to the Earl of Mar.[68]

On the valor of the English:

> Nor Death, nor Hell itself can keep them out,
> . . . Nor fortified redoubt.[69]

At other times this figure operates in a larger extent; and when the gentle reader is in expectation of some great image, he either finds it surprisingly imperfect or is presented with something very low or quite ridiculous: a surprise resembling that of a curious person in a cabinet of antique statues who beholds on the pedestal the names of Homer or Cato but, looking up, finds Homer without a head and nothing to be seen of Cato but his privy member. Such are these lines on a leviathan at sea:

> His motion works, and beats the oozy mud,
> And with its slime incorporates the flood,
> Till all th' encumbered, thick, fermenting stream

66. Anonymous [Pope].
67. Waller [Pope].
68. Anonymous [Pope].
69. Dennis on Namur [Pope].

> Does one vast pot of boiling ointment seem.
> Where'er he swims, he leaves along the lake
> Such frothy furrows, such a foamy track,
> That all the waters of the deep appear
> Hoary—with age, or gray with sudden fear.[70]

But perhaps even these are excelled by the ensuing:

> Now the resisted flames and fiery store,
> By winds assaulted, in wide forges roar,
> And raging seas flow down of melted ore.
> Sometimes they hear long iron bars removed,
> And to and fro huge heaps of cinders shoved.[71]

THE VULGAR

is also a species of the Diminishing; by this a spear flying in the air is compared to a boy whistling as he goes on an errand:

> The mighty Stuffa threw a massy spear,
> Which, with its errand pleased, sung through the air.[72]

A man raging with grief to a mastiff dog:

> I cannot stifle this gigantic woe,
> Nor on my raging grief a muzzle throw.[73]

And clouds big with water to a woman in great necessity:

> Distended with the waters in 'em pent,
> The clouds hang deep in air, but hang unrent.[74]

THE INFANTINE

This is when a poet grows so very simple as to think and talk like a child. I shall take my examples from the greatest master in this way. Hear how he fondles, like a mere stammerer:

> Little charm of placid mien,
> Miniature of beauty's queen
> Hither, British muse of mine,
> Hither, all ye Grecian nine,
> With the lovely Graces three,

70. Blackmore, *Job*, p. 197 [Pope].
71. *Prince Arthur*, p. 157 [Pope].
72. *Prince Arthur* [Pope].
73. *Job*, p. 41 [Pope].
74. Blackmore, *Job*, 1st ed. (1700), p. 115 (Steeves).

> And your pretty nurseling see.
> When the meadows next are seen,
> Sweet enamel, white and green.
> When again the lambkins play,
> Pretty sportlings full of May.
> Then the neck so white and round,
> (Little neck with brilliants bound).
> And thy gentleness of mind,
> (Gentle from a gentle kind) etc
> Happy thrice, and thrice again,
> Happiest he of happy men, etc.[75]

with the rest of those excellent lullabies of his composition.
How prettily he asks the sheep to teach him to bleat!

> Teach me to grieve with bleating moan, my sheep.[76]

Hear how a babe would reason on his nurse's death:

> That ever she could die! Oh most unkind!
> To die, and leave poor Colinet behind?
> And yet,—why blame I her?[77]

His shepherd reasons as much like an innocent, in love:

> I love in secret all a beauteous maid,
> And have my love in secret all repaid:
> This coming night she does reserve for me.[78]

The love of this maiden to him appears by her allowing him the
reserve of one night from her other lovers, which you see he
takes extremely kindly.

With no less simplicity does he suppose that shepherdesses
tear their hair and beat their breasts at their own deaths:

> Ye brighter maids, faint emblems of my fair,
> With looks cast down, and with disheveled hair,
> In bitter anguish beat your breasts, and moan
> Her death untimely, *as it were your own*.[79]

75. Ambrose Philips, on Miss C—— [Pope].
76. Philips, *Pastorals* [Pope].
77. Philips, *Pastorals* [Pope].
78. *Ibid.* [Pope].
79. *Ibid.* [Pope].

THE INANITY OR NOTHINGNESS

Of this the same author furnishes us with most beautiful
instances:

> Ah silly I, more silly than my sheep,
> (Which on the flow'ry plain I once did keep.)[80]
>
> To the grave Senate she could counsel give,
> (Which with astonishment they did receive.)[81]
>
> He whom loud cannon could not terrify,
> Falls (from the grandeur of his majesty.)[82]
>
> The noise returning with returning light,

What did it?

> Dispersed the silence, and dispelled the night.[83]
>
> The glories of proud London to survey,
> The sun himself shall rise—by break of day.[84]

THE EXPLETIVE,

admirably exemplified in the epithets of many authors.

> Th' umbrageous shadow, and the verdant green,
> The running current, and odorous fragrance,
> Cheer my lone solitude with joyous gladness.

THE MACROLOGY AND PLEONASM

are as generally coupled as a lean rabbit with a fat one; nor is it
a wonder, the superfluity of words and vacuity of sense being
just the same thing. I am pleased to see one of our greatest adversaries employ this figure:

> The growth of meadows, and the pride of fields.
> The food of armies, and support of wars.
> Refuse of swords, and gleanings of a fight.
> Lessen his numbers, and contract his host.
> Where'er his friends retire, or foes succeed.

80. Philips, *Pastorals* [Pope].
81. Philips on Queen Mary [Pope].
82. *Ibid.* [Pope].
83. Anonymous [Pope].
84. *Autor vetus* [Pope].

Covered with tempests, and in oceans drowned.[85]

Of all which the perfection is
THE TAUTOLOGY
Break through the billows, and—divide the main.[86]

In smoother numbers, and—in softer verse.[87]

Divide—and part—the severed world—in two.[88]

with ten thousand others equally musical and plentifully flowing through most of our celebrated modern poems.

CHAPTER XII
OF EXPRESSION, AND THE SEVERAL SORTS OF STYLE
OF THE PRESENT AGE

The expression is adequate when it is proportionably low to the profundity of the thought. It must not be always grammatical, lest it appear pedantic and ungentlemanly; nor too clear, for fear it become vulgar; for obscurity bestows a cast of the wonderful and throws an oracular dignity upon a piece which hath no meaning.

For example, sometimes use the wrong number: "The sword and pestilence at once *devours*," instead of "devour." Sometimes the wrong case: "And who more fit to soothe the God than *thee*,"[89] instead of "thou." And rather than say, "Thetis saw Achilles weep," she "heard" him weep.

We must be exceeding careful in two things: first, in the *choice* of low words; secondly, in the sober and orderly way of *ranging* them. Many of our poets are naturally blessed with this talent, insomuch that they are in the circumstance of that honest citizen who had made prose all his life without knowing it. Let verses run in this manner, just to be a vehicle to the words: (I take them from my last cited author, who, though otherwise by

85. *Campaign* [Pope]; by Addison; lines 199, 202, 192, 268, 168, 190.
86. Thomas Tickell, "The Royal Progress," in *Spectator* No. 620 (Steeves).
87. Tonson's *Miscellany*, duodecimo, 4th ed., IV, 291 [Pope].
88. *Ibid.*, VI, 121 [Pope]
89. Tickell, Homer's *Iliad*, I [Pope].

no means of our rank, seemed once in his life to have a mind to
be simple.)

> If not, a prize I will myself decree,
> From him, or him, or else perhaps from thee.[90]

> Full of days was he;
> Two ages past, he lived the third to see.[91]

> The King of forty Kings, and honored more
> By mighty Jove than e'er was King before.[92]

> That I may know, if thou my prayer deny,
> The most despised of all the gods am I.[93]

> Then let my mother once be ruled by me,
> Though much more wise than I pretend to be.[94]

Or these of the same hand:

> I leave the arts of poetry and verse
> To them that practice them with more success:
> Of greater truths I now prepare to tell,
> And so at once, dear friend and Muse, farewell.[95]

Sometimes a single word will familiarize a poetical idea, as
where a ship set on fire owes all the spirit of the Bathos to one
choice word that ends the line:

> And his scorched ribs the hot contagion *fried*.[96]

And in that description of a world in ruins:

> Should the whole frame of Nature round him break,
> He unconcerned would hear the mighty *crack*.[97]

So also in these:

90. Tickell, Homer's *Iliad*, I, p. 11 [Pope].
91. *Idem*, p. 17 [Pope].
92. P. 19 [Pope].
93. P. 34 [Pope].
94. P. 38 [Pope].
95. Tonson's *Miscellany*, duodecimo, 4th ed., IV, 292 [Pope]; the concluding lines of Addison's "An Account of the Greatest English Poets."
96. *Prince Arthur*, p. 151 [Pope].
97. Tonson's *Miscellany*, VI, 119 [Pope]; from Addison's "Horace, Ode
III, Book III."

Beasts tame and savage to the river's brink
Come from the fields and wild abodes—*to drink*.98

Frequently two or three words will do it effectually:

He from the clouds does the *sweet liquor squeeze,*
That cheers the *forest and the garden* trees.99

It is also useful to employ technical terms, which estrange your style from the great and general ideas of Nature; and the higher your subject is, the lower should you search into mechanics for your expression. If you describe the garment of an angel, say that his "linen" was "finely spun" and "bleached on the happy plains."100 Call an army of angels "angelic cuirassiers,"101 and if you have occasion to mention a number of misfortunes, style them

Fresh *troops* of pains, and *regimented* woes.102

Style is divided by the rhetoricians into the proper and the figured. Of the figured we have already treated, and the proper is what our authors have nothing to do with. Of styles we shall mention only the principal which owe to the Moderns either their chief improvement or entire invention.

1. THE FLORID,

than which none is more proper to the Bathos, as flowers which are the lowest of vegetables are the most gaudy and do many times grow in great plenty at the bottom of ponds and ditches.

A fine writer in this kind presents you with the following posy:

The groves appear all dressed with wreaths of flowers,
And from their leaves drop aromatic showers,
Whose fragrant heads in mystic twines above,
Exchanged their sweets, and mixed with thousand kisses,
As if the willing branches strove
To beautify and shade the grove—103

98. *Job,* p. 263 [Pope].
99. *Idem,* p. 264 [Pope].
100. *Prince Arthur,* p. 19 [Pope].
101. *Ibid.,* p. 239 [Pope].
102. *Job,* p. 86 [Pope].
103. Behn's *Poems,* p. 2 [Pope].

(which indeed most branches do.) But this is still excelled by our Laureate:

> Branches in branches twined compose the grove,
> And shoot and spread, and blossom into love.
> The trembling palms their mutual vows repeat,
> And bending poplars bending poplars meet.
> The distant platans seem to press more nigh,
> And to the sighing alders, alders sigh.[104]

Hear also our Homer:

> His robe of state is formed of light refined,
> An endless train of lustre spreads behind.
> His throne's of bright compacted glory made,
> With pearl celestial, and with gems inlaid:
> Whence floods of joy and seas of splendor flow,
> On all th' angelic gazing throng below.[105]

2. THE PERT STYLE.

This does in as peculiar a manner become the low in wit as a pert air does the low in stature. Mr. Thomas Brown, the author of the *London Spy*,[106] and all the spies and trips[107] in general are herein to be diligently studied; in verse, Mr. Cibber's prologues.

But the beauty and energy of it is never so conspicuous as when it is employed in modernizing and adapting to the taste of the times the works of the Ancients. This we rightly phrase "doing them into English" and "making them English," two expressions of great propriety, the one denoting our neglect of the manner how, the other the force and compulsion with which it is brought about. It is by virtue of this style that Tacitus talks like a coffee-house politician, Josephus like the British Gazetteer, Tully is as short and smart as Seneca or Mr. Asgill, Marcus Aurelius is excellent at snipsnap,[108] and honest Thomas à Kempis as prim and polite as any preacher at court.

---

104. *Guardian*, duodecimo, 127 [Pope]; "our Laureate" is Eusden.
105. Blackmore, *Psalm 104* [Pope].
106. Edward Ward
107. Accounts of journeys.
108. Repartee.

3. THE ALAMODE STYLE,

which is fine by being *new* and has this happiness attending it, that it is as durable and extensive as the poem itself. Take some examples of it, in the description of the sun in a mourning coach upon the death of Q[ueen] Mary:

> See Phoebus now, as once for Phaeton,
> Has masked his face, and put deep mourning on;
> Dark clouds his sable chariot do surround,
> And the dull steeds stalk o'er the melancholy round.[109]

Of Prince Arthur's soldiers drinking:

> While rich Burgundian wine, and bright Champagne,
> Chase from their minds the terrors of the main.[110]

(Whence we also learn that Burgundy and Champagne make a man on shore despise a storm at sea.)
Of the Almighty encamping his regiments:

> He sunk a vast capacious deep,
> Where he his liquid regiments does keep;
> Thither the waves file off, and make their way,
> To form the mighty body of the sea;
> Where they encamp, and in their station stand,
> Entrenched in works of rock, and lines of sand.[111]

Of two armies on the point of engaging:

> Yon armies are the cards which both must play;
> At least come off a saver if you may:
> Throw boldly at the sum the gods have set;
> These on your side will all their fortunes bet.[112]

All perfectly agreeable to the present customs and best fashions of this our metropolis.

But the principal branch of the Alamode is the PRURIENT, a style greatly advanced and honored of late by the practice of persons of the first quality and, by the encouragement of the ladies, not unsuccessfully introduced even into the drawing-room.

109. Ambrose Philips [Pope].
110. *Prince Arthur*, p. 16 [Pope].
111. Blackmore, *Psalm 104*, p. 261 [Pope].
112. Lee, *Sophonisba* [Pope].

Indeed its incredible progress and conquests may be compared to those of the great Sesostris[113] and are everywhere known by the same marks, the images of the genital parts of men or women. It consists wholly of metaphors drawn from two most fruitful sources or springs, the very Bathos of the human body, that is to say * * * * and * * * * * * * * * * * * * *Hiatus magnus lachrymabilis*[114] *. And selling of bargains, and *double entendre*, and Χιββέϱισμος and 'Ολδφίελδισμος,[115] all derived from the said sources.

4. THE FINICAL,

which consists of the most curious, affected, mincing metaphors and partakes of the last mentioned. As this, of a brook dried by the sun:

> Won by the summer's importuning ray,
> Th' eloping stream did from her channel stray,
> And with enticing sunbeams stole away.[116]

Of an easy death:

> When watchful death shall on his harvest look,
> And see thee ripe with age, invite the hook;
> He'll gently cut thy bending stalk, and thee
> Lay kindly in the grave, his granary.[117]

Of trees in a storm:

> Oaks with extended arms the winds defy,
> The tempest sees their strength, and sighs, and passes by.[118]

Of water simmering over the fire:

> The sparkling flames raise water to a smile,
> Yet the pleased liquor pines, and lessens all the while.[119]

113. A legendary king of Egypt.
114. "A lamentable large gap in the text."
115. "Cibberism and Oldfieldism"; a reference to Colley Cibber and Mrs. Anne Oldfield, the actress.
116. Blackmore, *Job*, p. 26 [Pope].
117. *Ibid.*, p. 23 [Pope].
118. Dennis [Pope].
119. Anonymous, in Tonson's *Miscellany*, Part VI, p. 234 [Pope].

5. Lastly I shall place THE CUMBROUS, which moves heavily under a load of metaphors and draws after it a long train of words. And the BUSKIN, or Stately, frequently and with great felicity mixed with the former. For as the first is the proper engine to depress what is high, so is the second to raise what is base and low to a ridiculous visibility. When both these can be done at once, then is the Bathos in perfection; as when a man is set with his head downward and his breech upright, his degradation is complete: one end of him is as high as ever, only that end is the wrong one. Will not every true lover of the Profund be delighted to behold the most vulgar and low actions of life exalted in this manner?

Who knocks at the door?

> For whom thus rudely pleads my loud-tongued gate,
> That he may enter?

See who is there.

> Advance the fringed curtains of thy eyes,
> And tell me who comes yonder.[120]

Shut the door.

> The wooden guardian of our privacy
> Quick on its axle turn.

Bring my clothes.

> Bring me what Nature, tailor to the bear,
> To man himself denied: she gave me cold,
> But would not give me clothes.

Light the fire.

> Bring forth some remnant of Promethean theft,
> Quick to expand th' inclement air congealed
> By Boreas's rude breath.

Snuff the candle.

> Yon luminary amputation needs,
> Thus shall you save its half-extinguished life.

120. *Tempest* [Pope].

Open the letter.

Wax! render up thy trust.[121]

Uncork the bottle and chip the bread.

Apply thine engine to the spungy door,
Set Bacchus from his glassy prison free,
And Strip white Ceres of her nut-brown coat.

APPENDIX
CHAPTER XIII
A PROJECT FOR THE ADVANCEMENT OF THE BATHOS

Thus have I (my dear countrymen) with incredible pains and diligence discovered the hidden sources of the Bathos, or, as I may say, broke open the abysses of this Great Deep. And having now established the good and wholesome laws, what remains but that all true Moderns with their utmost might do proceed to put the same in execution? In order whereto, I think I shall in the second place highly deserve of my country by proposing such a scheme as may facilitate this great end.

As our number is confessedly far superior to that of the enemy, there seems nothing wanting but unanimity among ourselves. It is therefore humbly offered that all and every individual of the Bathos do enter into a firm Association and incorporate into one regular body, whereof every member, even the meanest, will some way contribute to the support of the whole, in like manner as the weakest reeds, when joined in one bundle, become infrangible. To which end our art ought to be put upon the same foot with other arts of this age. The vast improvement of modern manufactures ariseth from their being divided into several branches and parcelled out to several trades. For instance, in clock-making one artist makes the balance, another the spring, another the crown-wheels, a fourth the case, and the principal workman puts all together. To this economy we owe the perfection of our modern watches, and doubtless we also might that of our modern poetry and rhetoric, were the several parts branched out in the like manner.

121. Theobald, *Double Distress* [Pope]; i.e., *Double Falsehood*.

Nothing is more evident than that divers persons, no other way remarkable, have each a strong disposition to the formation of some particular trope or figure. Aristotle saith that the hyperbole is an ornament of speech fit for young men of quality; accordingly we find in those gentlemen a wonderful propensity toward it, which is marvelously improved by traveling. Soldiers also and seamen are very happy in the same figure. The periphrasis or circumlocution is the peculiar talent of country farmers, the proverb and apologue of old men at their clubs, the ellipsis or speech by half-words of ministers and politicians, the aposiopesis of courtiers, the litotes[122] or diminution of ladies, whisperers, and backbiters, and the anadiplosis of common criers and hawkers, who by redoubling the same words persuade people to buy their oysters, green hastings,[123] or new ballads. Epithets may be found in great plenty at Billingsgate, sarcasm and irony learned upon the water, and the epiphonema or exclamation frequently from the Bear-garden and as frequently from the "Hear him" of the House of Commons.

Now, each man applying his whole time and genius upon his particular figure would doubtless attain to perfection; and when each became incorporated and sworn into the Society (as hath been proposed), a poet or orator would have no more to do but to send to the particular traders in each kind: to the metaphorist for his allegories, to the simile-maker for his comparisons, to the ironist for his sarcasms, to the apothegmatist for his sentences, etc., whereby a dedication or speech would be composed in a moment, the superior artist having nothing to do but to put together all the materials.

I therefore propose that there be contrived with all convenient dispatch, at the public expense, a Rhetorical Chest of Drawers, consisting of three stories, the highest for the deliberative, the middle for the demonstrative, and the lowest for the judicial. These shall be divided into *loci,* or places, being repositories for matter and argument in the several kinds of oration or writing; and every drawer shall again be subdivided into cells, resembling

122. Misprinted *littole* in the first edition.
123. Early-ripening fruits or vegetables.

those of cabinets for rarities. The apartment for peace or war, and that of the liberty of the press, may in a very few days be filled with several arguments *perfectly new;* and the Vituperative Partition will as easily be replenished with a most choice collection, entirely of the growth and manufacture of the present age. Every composer will soon be taught the use of this cabinet and how to manage all the registers of it, which will be drawn out much in the manner of those of an organ.

The keys of it must be kept in honest hands, by some reverend prelate or valiant officer of unquestioned loyalty and affection to every present establishment in Church and State, which will sufficiently guard against any mischief which might otherwise be apprehended from it.

And, being lodged in such hands, it may be at discretion let out by the day to several great orators in both Houses, from whence it is to be hoped much profit or gain will also accrue to our society.

CHAPTER XIV

HOW TO MAKE DEDICATIONS, PANEGYRICS, OR SATIRES, AND OF THE
COLORS OF HONORABLE AND DISHONORABLE

Now of what necessity the foregoing project may prove will appear from this single consideration, that nothing is of equal consequence to the success of our works as speed and dispatch. Great pity it is that solid brains are not, like other solid bodies, constantly endowed with a velocity in sinking proportioned to their heaviness. For it is with the flowers of the Bathos as with those of Nature, which, if the careful gardener brings not hastily to the market in the morning, must unprofitably perish and wither before night. And of all our productions none is so short-lived as the Dedication and Panegyric, which are often but the praise of a day and become, by the next, utterly useless, improper, indecent, and false. This is the more to be lamented, inasmuch as they are the very two sorts whereon in a manner depends that gain or profit which must still be remembered to be the whole end of our writers and speakers.

We shall therefore employ this chapter in showing the quickest method of composing them; after which we will teach a short way to epic poetry. And these being confessedly the works of most importance and difficulty, it is presumed we may leave the rest to each author's own learning or practice.

First of Panegyric: every man is honorable who is so by law, custom, or title; the public are better judges of what is honorable than private men. The virtues of great men, like those of plants, are inherent in them whether they are exerted or not; and the more strongly inherent the less they are exerted, as a man is the more rich the less he spends.

All great ministers, without either private or economical virtue, are virtuous by their posts: liberal and generous upon the public money, provident upon parliamentary supplies, just by paying public interest, courageous and magnanimous by the fleets and armies, magnificent upon the public expenses, and prudent by public success. They have by their office a right to a share of the public stock of virtues; besides, they are by prescription immemorial invested in all the celebrated virtues of their predecessors in the same stations, especially those of their own ancestors.

As to what are commonly called the "colors" of honorable and dishonorable, they are various in different countries; in this they are blue, green, and red.[124] But forasmuch as the duty we owe to the public doth often require that we should put some things in a strong light and throw a shade over others, I shall explain the method of turning a vicious man into a hero.

The first and chief rule is the Golden Rule of Transformation, which consists in converting vices into their *bordering* virtues. A man who is a spendthrift and will not pay a just debt may have his injustice transformed into liberality; cowardice may be metamorphosed into prudence; intemperance into good nature and good fellowship: corruption into patriotism; and lewdness into tenderness and facility.

The second is the Rule of Contraries. It is certain the less a man is endued with any virtue the more need he has to have

124. The orders of the Garter, the Bath, and the Thistle; Pope puns on the meaning of color as rhetorical mode.

84 LITERARY CRITICISM OF POPE

it plentifully bestowed, especially those good qualities of which the world generally believes he hath none at all. For who will thank a man for giving him that which he *has*?

The reverse of these precepts will serve for satire, wherein we are ever to remark that whoso loseth his place or becomes out of favor with the government hath forfeited his share of public praise and honor. Therefore the truly public-spirited writer ought in duty to strip him whom the government has stripped, which is the real poetical justice of this age. For a full collection of topics and epithets to be used in the praise and dispraise of ministerial and unministerial persons, I refer to our Rhetorical Cabinet, concluding with an earnest exhortation to all my brethren to observe the precepts here laid down, the neglect of which hath cost some of them their ears in a pillory.

CHAPTER XV
A RECEIPT TO MAKE AN EPIC POEM[125]

An epic poem, the critics agree, is the greatest work human nature is capable of. They have already laid down many mechanical rules for compositions of this sort, but at the same time they cut off almost all undertakers from the possibility of ever performing them; for the first qualification they unanimously require in a poet is a genius. I shall here endeavor (for the benefit of my countrymen) to make it manifest that epic poems may be made *without a genius,* nay without learning or much reading. This must necessarily be of great use to all those who confess they never read, and of whom the world is convinced they never learn. What Molière observes of making a dinner, that any man can do it with money and if a professed cook cannot do it without he has his art for nothing, the same may be said of making a poem; 'tis easily brought about by him that *has* a genius, but the skill lies in doing it without one. In pursuance of this end, I shall present the reader with a plain and certain recipe by which any author in the Bathos may be qualified for this grand performance.

125. First published as *Guardian* No. 78 (June 10, 1713).

For the Fable.

Take out of any old poem, history-book, romance, or legend (for instance, Geoffrey of Monmouth or Don Belianis of Greece) those parts of story which afford most scope for long descriptions. Put these pieces together, and throw all the adventures you fancy into one tale. Then take a hero, whom you may choose for the sound of his name, and put him into the midst of these adventures. There let him *work*, for twelve books, at the end of which you may take him out, ready prepared to conquer or to marry, it being necessary that the conclusion of an epic poem be fortunate.

To make an Episode.

Take any remaining adventure of your former collection in which you could no way involve your hero, or any unfortunate accident that was too good to be thrown away, and it will be of use applied to any other person, who may be lost and *evaporate* in the course of the work without the least damage to the composition.

For the Moral and Allegory.

These you may extract out of the Fable afterwards, at your leisure. Be sure you *strain* them sufficiently.

For the Manners.

For those of the hero, take all the best qualities you can find in the most celebrated heroes of antiquity; if they will not be reduced to a consistency, lay 'em all on a heap upon him. But be sure they are qualities which your Patron would be thought to have; and, to prevent any mistake which the world may be subject to, select from the alphabet those capital letters that compose his name and set them at the head of a dedication before your poem. However, do not absolutely observe the exact quantity of these virtues, it not being determined whether or no it be necessary for the hero of a poem to be an honest man. For the under-characters, gather them from Homer and Virgil, and change the names as occasion serves.

For the Machines.

Take of deities, male and female, as many as you can use.

Separate them into two equal parts, and keep Jupiter in the middle. Let Juno put him in a ferment, and Venus mollify him. Remember on all occasions to make use of volatile Mercury. If you have need of devils, draw them out of Milton's Paradise, and extract your spirits from Tasso. The use of these machines is evident; for since no epic poem can possibly subsist without them, the wisest way is to reserve them for your greatest necessities. When you cannot extricate your hero by any human means, or yourself by your own wit, seek relief from heaven, and the gods will do your business very readily. This is according to the direct prescription of Horace in his *Art of Poetry:*

Nec deus intersit, nisi dignus vindice nodus inciderit.

That is to say, "A poet should never call upon the gods for their assistance, but when he is in great perplexity."[126]

For the Descriptions.

For a Tempest: Take Eurus, Zephyr, Auster, and Boreas, and cast them together in one verse. Add to these of rain, lightning and of thunder (the loudest you can) *quantum sufficit.*[127] Mix your clouds and billows well together till they foam, and thicken your description here and there with a quicksand. Brew your tempest well in your head before you set it a-blowing.

For a Battle: Pick a large quantity of images and descriptions from Homer's *Iliads,* with a spice or two of Virgil, and if there remain any overplus, you may lay them by for a Skirmish. Season it well with similes, and it will make an excellent battle.

For a Burning Town: If such a description be necessary (because it is certain there is one in Virgil), old Troy is ready burnt to your hands. But if you fear that would be thought borrowed, a chapter or two of the Theory of the Conflagration,[128] well circumstanced and done into verse, will be a good succedaneum.

As for similes and metaphors, they may be found all over

126. *Ars Poetica,* 191–192.
127. "As much as is necessary."
128. Thomas Burnet's *Sacred Theory of the Earth.*

the creation; the most ignorant may gather them, but the danger
is in applying them. For this advise with your Bookseller.

CHAPTER XVI
A PROJECT FOR THE ADVANCEMENT OF THE STAGE

It may be thought that we should not wholly omit the drama,
which makes so great and so lucrative a part of poetry. But this
province is so well taken care of by the present managers of
the theatre that it is perfectly needless to suggest to them any
other methods than they have already practised for the advancement of the Bathos.

Here, therefore, in the name of all our brethren, let me
return our sincere and humble thanks to the Most August Mr.
B—t—n B—th, the Most Serene Mr. W—ll—m W—lks, and the
Most Undaunted Mr. C—ll—y C—bb—r,[129] of whom, let it be
known when the people of this age shall be ancestors, and to
all the succession of our successors, that to this present day they
continue to outdo even their own outdoings. And when the inevit-
able hand of sweeping time shall have brushed off all the works
of today, may this testimony of a co-temporary critic to their
fame be extended as far as tomorrow!

Yet, if to so wise an administration it be possible anything
can be added, it is that more ample and comprehensive scheme
which Mr. D—nn—s and Mr. Gildon (the two greatest critics and
reformers then living) made public in the year 1720 in a project
signed with their names and dated the 2d of February. I cannot
better conclude than by presenting the reader with the substance
of it.[130]

1. It is proposed that the two theaters be incorporated into
one company; that the Royal Academy of Music be added to
them as an Orchestra; and that Mr. Figg with his prize fighters
and Violante with the rope-dancers be admitted in partnership.

2. That a spacious building be erected at the public expense,

129. Barton Booth, Robert Wilks, and Colley Cibber, actor-managers at
Drury Lane. Wilks' first name was given correctly in later editions.
130. What follows appears to be a burlesque of a proposal by Dennis
and Gildon which is no longer extant.

capable of containing at least ten thousand spectators, which is become absolutely necessary by the great addition of children and nurses to the audience since the new entertainments. That there be a stage as large as the Athenian, which was near ninety thousand geometrical paces square, and separate divisions for the two Houses of Parliament, my lords the Judges, the honorable the Directors of the Academy, and the Court of Aldermen, who shall all have their places frank.

3. If Westminster Hall be not allotted to this service (which by reason of its proximity to the two chambers of Parliament above mentioned seems not altogether improper), it is left to the wisdom of the nation whether Somerset House may not be demolished and a theater built upon that site, which lies convenient to receive spectators from the county of Surrey, who may be wafted thither by water-carriage, esteemed by all projectors the cheapest whatsoever. To this may be added that the river Thames may in the readiest manner convey those eminent personages from courts beyond the seas, who may be drawn either by curiosity to behold some of our most celebrated pieces or by affection to see their countrymen the harlequins and eunuchs, of which convenient notice may be given for two or three months before in the public prints.

4. That the theater abovesaid be environed with a fair quadrangle of buildings fitted for the accommodation of decayed critics and poets, out of whom six of the most aged (their age to be computed from the year wherein their first work was published) shall be elected to manage the affairs of the society, provided nevertheless that the Laureate for the time being may be always one. The Head or President over all (to prevent disputes, but too frequent among the learned) shall be the oldest poet and critic to be found in the whole island.

5. The male players are to be lodged in the garrets of the said quadrangle and to attend the persons of the poets dwelling under them by brushing their apparel, drawing on their shoes, and the like. The actresses are to make their beds and wash their linen.

6. A large room shall be set apart for a library, to consist of

all the modern dramatic poems and all the criticisms extant. In the midst of this room shall be a round table for the Council of Six to sit and deliberate on the merits of plays. The majority shall determine the dispute; and if it should happen that three and three should be of each side, the President shall have a casting voice, unless where the contention may run so high as to require a decision by single combat.

7. It may be convenient to place the Council of Six in some conspicuous situation in the theater, where, after the manner usually practiced by composers in music, they may give signs (before settled and agreed upon) of dislike or approbation. In consequence of these signs the whole audience shall be required to *clap* or *hiss*, that the town may learn certainly when and how far they ought to be pleased.

8. It is submitted whether it would not be proper to distinguish the Council of Six by some particular habit or gown of an honorable shape and color, to which might be added a square cap and a white wand.

9. That to prevent unmarried actresses making away with their infants, a competent provision be allowed for the nurture of them, who shall for that reason be deemed the Children of the Society; and that they may be educated according to the genius of their parents, the said actresses shall declare upon oath (as far as their memory will allow) the true names and qualities of their several fathers. A private gentleman's son shall at the public expense be brought up a page to attend the Council of Six. A more ample provision shall be made for the son of a poet; and a greater still for the son of a critic.

10. If it be discovered that any actress is got with child, during the interludes of any play wherein she hath a part, it shall be reckoned a neglect of her business, and she shall forfeit accordingly. If any actor for the future shall commit murder, except upon the stage, he shall be left to the laws of the land; the like is to be understood of robbery and theft. In all other cases, particularly in those of debt, it is proposed that this, like the other courts of Whitehall and St. James's, may be held a place of privilege. And whereas it has been found that an obligation to

satisfy paltry creditors has been a discouragement to men of letters, if any person of quality or others shall send for any poet or critic of this Society to any remote quarter of the town, the said poet or critic shall freely pass and repass without being liable to an arrest.

11. The aforementioned scheme in its several regulations may be supported by profits arising from every third night throughout the year. And as it would be hard to suppose that so many persons could live without any food (though from the former course of their lives a very little will be sufficient), the masters of calculation will, we believe, agree that out of those profits the said persons might be subsisted in a sober and decent manner. We will venture to affirm farther that not only the proper magazines of thunder and lightning, but paint, diet-drinks, spitting-pots, and all other necessaries of life may in like manner fairly be provided for.

12. If some of the articles may at first view seem liable to objections, particularly those that give so vast a power to the Council of Six (which is indeed larger than any intrusted to the great officers of state), this may be obviated by swearing those six persons of his Majesty's Privy Council and obliging them to pass everything of moment *previously* at that most honorable board.

Vale & Fruere.

MAR. SCRIB.

CRITICISM OF PASTORAL

A Discourse on Pastoral Poetry (1704)[1]

There are not, I believe, a greater number of any sort of verses than of those which are called pastorals, nor a smaller than of those which are truly so. It therefore seems necessary to give some account of this kind of poem, and it is my design to comprise in this short paper the substance of those numerous dissertations the critics have made on the subject, without omitting any of their rules in my own favor. You will also find some points reconciled about which they seem to differ and a few remarks which I think have escaped their observation.

The original of poetry is ascribed to that age which succeeded the creation of the world; and as the keeping of flocks seems to have been the first employment of mankind, the most ancient sort of poetry was probably pastoral. 'Tis natural to imagine that, the leisure of those ancient shepherds admitting and inviting some diversion, none was so proper to that solitary and sedentary life as singing, and that in their songs they took occasion to celebrate their own felicity. From hence a poem was invented, and afterwards improved to a perfect image of that happy time, which by giving us an esteem for the virtues of a former age might recommend them to the present. And since the life of shepherds was attended with more tranquillity than any other rural employment, the poets chose to introduce their persons, from whom it received the name of pastoral.

A pastoral is an imitation of the action of a shepherd, or one considered under that character. The form of this imitation is dramatic, or narrative, or mixed of both; the fable simple, the manners not too polite nor too rustic. The thoughts are plain, yet admit a little quickness and passion, but that short and flowing; the expression humble, yet as pure as the language will afford; neat, but not florid; easy, and yet lively. In short, the

1. Written at sixteen years of age [Pope].

93

fable, manners, thoughts, and expressions are full of the greatest simplicity in nature.

The complete character of this poem consists in simplicity, brevity, and delicacy, the two first of which render an eclogue natural, and the last delightful.

If we would copy Nature, it may be useful to take this idea along with us, that pastoral is an image of what they call the Golden Age. So that we are not to describe our shepherds as shepherds at this day really are, but as they may be conceived then to have been, when the best of men followed the employment. To carry this resemblance yet farther, it would not be amiss to give these shepherds some skill in astronomy, as far as it may be useful to that sort of life. And an air of piety to the gods should shine through the poem, which so visibly appears in all the works of antiquity. And it ought to preserve some relish of the old way of writing; the connections should be loose, the narrations and descriptions short, and the periods concise. Yet it is not sufficient that the sentences only be brief; the whole eclogue should be so too. For we cannot suppose poetry in those days to have been the business of men, but their recreation at vacant hours.

But with a respect to the present age, nothing more conduces to make these composures natural than when some knowledge in rural affairs is discovered. This may be made to appear rather done by chance than on design, and sometimes is best shown by inference, lest by too much study to seem natural we destroy that easy simplicity from whence arises the delight. For what is inviting in this sort of poetry proceeds not so much from the idea of that business as of the tranquillity of a country life.

We must therefore use some illusion to render a pastoral delightful; and this consists in exposing the best side only of a shepherd's life and in concealing its miseries. Nor is it enough to introduce shepherds discoursing together in a natural way; but a regard must be had to the subject, that it contain some particular beauty in itself and that it be different in every eclogue. Besides, in each of them a designed scene or prospect is to be presented to our view, which should likewise have its variety.

This variety is obtained in a great degree by frequent comparisons, drawn from the most agreeable objects of the country; by interrogations to things inanimate; by beautiful digressions, but those short; sometimes by insisting a little on circumstances; and lastly by elegant turns on the words, which render the numbers extremely sweet and pleasing. As for the numbers themselves, though they are properly of the heroic measure, they should be the smoothest, the most easy and flowing imaginable.

It is by rules like these that we ought to judge of pastoral. And since the instructions given for any art are to be delivered as that art is in perfection, they must of necessity be derived from those in whom it is acknowledged so to be. 'Tis therefore from the practice of Theocritus and Virgil (the only undisputed authors of pastoral) that the critics have drawn the foregoing notions concerning it.

Theocritus excels all others in nature and simplicity. The subjects of his *Idyllia* are purely pastoral, but he is not so exact in his persons, having introduced reapers and fishermen as well as shepherds. He is apt to be too long in his descriptions, of which that of the cup in the first pastoral is a remarkable instance. In the manners he seems a little defective, for his swains are sometimes abusive and immodest and perhaps too much inclining to rusticity: for instance, in his fourth and fifth *Idyllia*. But 'tis enough that all others learned their excellencies from him and that his dialect alone has a secret charm in it which no other could ever attain.

Virgil, who copies Theocritus, refines upon his original; and in all points where judgment is principally concerned, he is much superior to his master. Though some of his subjecets are not pastoral in themselves but only seem to be such, they have a wonderful variety in them which the Greek was a stranger to. He exceeds him in regularity and brevity and falls short of him in nothing but simplicity and propriety of style, the first of which perhaps was the fault of his age and the last of his language.

Among the moderns, their success has been greatest who have most endeavored to make these ancients their pattern. The most considerable genius appears in the famous Tasso and our Spenser.

Tasso in his *Aminta* has as far excelled all the pastoral writers as in his *Gierusalemme*[2] he has outdone the epic poets of his country. But as this piece seems to have been the original of a new sort of poem, the pastoral comedy, in Italy, it cannot so well be considered as a copy of the ancients. Spenser's *Calendar*, in Mr. Dryden's opinion,[3] is the most complete work of this kind which any nation has produced ever since the time of Virgil. Not but that he may be thought imperfect in some few points. His eclogues are somewhat too long, if we compare them with the ancients. He is sometimes too allegorical and treats of matters of religion in a pastoral style as Mantuan[4] had done before him. He has employed the lyric measure, which is contrary to the practice of the old poets. His stanza is not still[5] the same, nor always well chosen. This last may be the reason his expression is sometimes not concise enough; for the tetrastic has obliged him to extend his sense to the length of four lines, which would have been more closely confined in the couplet.

In the manners, thoughts, and characters, he comes near to Theocritus himself, though, notwithstanding all the care he has taken, he is certainly inferior in his dialect. For the Doric had its beauty and propriety in the time of Theocritus; it was used in part of Greece and frequent in the mouths of many of the greatest persons; whereas the old English and country phrases of Spenser were either entirely obsolete or spoken only by people of the lowest condition. As there is a difference between simplicity and rusticity, so the expression of simple thoughts should be plain, but not clownish. The addition he has made of a calendar to his eclogues is very beautiful, since by this, besides the general moral of innocence and simplicity which is common to other authors of pastoral, he has one peculiar to himself; he compares human life to the several seasons and at once exposes to his readers a view of the great and little worlds, in their various

2. Tasso's *Jerusalem Delivered;* for further comments by Pope on *Aminta*, see above, p. 34.
3. Dedication to Virgil's *Eclogues* [Pope].
4. Baptista Mantuanus (1448–1516), who wrote Latin pastorals.
5. Always.

changes and aspects. Yet the scrupulous division of his pastorals into months has obliged him either to repeat the same description in other words for three months together or, when it was exhausted before, entirely to omit it: whence it comes to pass that some of his eclogues (as the sixth, eighth, and tenth, for example) have nothing but their titles to distinguish them. The reason is evident, because the year has not that variety in it to furnish every month with a particular description, as it may every season.

Of the following eclogues I shall only say that these four comprehend all the subjects which the critics upon Theocritus and Virgil will allow to be fit for pastoral; that they have as much variety of description, in respect of the several seasons, as Spenser's; that, in order to add to this variety, the several times of the day are observed, the rural employments in each season or time of day, and the rural scenes or places proper to such employments, not without some regard to the several ages of man and the different passions proper to each age.

But, after all, if they have any merit it is to be attributed to some good old authors, whose works as I had leisure to study, so I hope I have not wanted care to imitate.

The Guardian No. 40

MONDAY, APRIL 27, 1713

Corydon and Thyrsis had driven their flocks together.
From that day it is Corydon, Corydon with us.[1]

I designed to have troubled the reader with no farther discourses of pastorals, but, being informed that I am taxed of partiality in not mentioning an author whose eclogues are published in the same volume with Mr. Philips's, I shall employ this paper in observations upon him, written in the free spirit of criticism and without apprehension of offending that gentleman, whose character it is that he takes the greatest care of his works before they are published and has the least concern for them afterwards.

I have laid it down as the first rule of pastoral that its idea should be taken from the manners of the Golden Age and the moral formed upon the representation of innocence; 'tis therefore plain that any deviations from that design degrade a poem from being true pastoral. In this view it will appear that Virgil can only have two of his eclogues allowed to be such. His first and ninth must be rejected because they describe the ravages of armies and oppressions of the innocent; Corydon's criminal passion for Alexis throws out the second; the calumny and railing in the third are not proper to that state of concord; the eighth represents unlawful ways of procuring love by echantments and introduces a shepherd whom an inviting precipice tempts to self-murder. As to the fourth, sixth, and tenth, they are given up by Heinsius, Salmasius, Rapin,[2] and the critics in general. They

1. *Compulerante greges Corydon et Thyrsis in unum.*
   Ex illo Corydon, Corydon est tempore nobis.
Virgil, *Eclogue* VII, 2, 70, trans. Fairclough. The eclogue is a contest between two shepherd-poets.
2. See Rapin, *De Carmine Pastorali*, Part 3 [Pope].

likewise observe that but eleven of all the *Idyllia* of Theocritus
are to be admitted as pastorals; and even out of that number the
greater part will be excluded for one or other of the reasons
above mentioned. So that when I remarked in a former paper
that Virgil's eclogues, taken all together, are rather select poems
than pastorals, I might have said the same thing, with no less
truth, of Theocritus. The reason of this I take to be yet unobserved by the critics, viz. they never meant them all for pastorals.
Which it is plain Philips hath done, and in that particular
excelled both Theocritus and Virgil.

As simplicity is the distinguishing characteristic of pastoral,
Virgil hath been thought guilty of too courtly a style; his language
is perfectly pure, and he often forgets he is among peasants. I
have frequently wondered that since he was so conversant in the
writings of Ennius,[3] he had not imitated the rusticity of the Doric
as well, by the help of the old obsolete Roman language, as
Philips hath by the antiquated English. For example, might he
not have said *quoi* instead of *cui, quoijum* for *cujum, volt* for
vult, etc., as well as our Modern hath *welladay* for *alas, whilome*
for *of old, make mock* for *deride*, and *witless younglings* for
simple lambs, etc., by which means he had attained as much of
the air of Theocritus as Philips hath of Spenser?

Mr. Pope hath fallen into the same error with Virgil. His
clowns do not converse in all the simplicity proper to the country; his names are borrowed from Theocritus and Virgil, which
are improper to the scene of his pastorals. He introduces Daphnis,
Alexis, and Thyrsis on British plains as Virgil had done before
him on the Mantuan; whereas Philips, who hath the strictest
regard to propriety, makes a choice of names peculiar to the
country and more agreeable to a reader of delicacy, such as
Hobbinol, Lobbin, Cuddy, and Colin Clout.

So easy as pastoral writing may seem (in the simplicity we
have described it), yet it requires great reading, both of the
Ancients and Moderns, to be a master of it. Philips hath given us
manifest proofs of his knowledge of books; it must be confessed
his competitor hath imitated some single thoughts of the Ancients

3. Quintus Ennius (239–170 B.C.), ancient Latin poet.

well enough, if we consider he had not the happiness of an university education; but he hath dispersed them, here and there, without that order and method which Mr. Philips observes, whose whole third pastoral is an instance how well he hath studied the fifth of Virgil and how judiciously reduced Virgil's thoughts to the standard of pastoral, as his contention of Colin Clout and the nightingale shows with what exactness he hath imitated Strada.[4]

When I remarked it as a principal fault to introduce fruits and flowers of a foreign growth in descriptions where the scene lies in our country, I did not design that observation should extend also to animals or the sensitive life, for Philips hath with great judgment described wolves in England in his first pastoral. Nor would I have a poet slavishly confine himself (as Mr. Pope hath done) to one particular season of the year, one certain time of the day, and one unbroken scene in each eclogue. 'Tis plain Spenser neglected this pedantry, who in his pastoral of November mentions the mournful song of the nightingale: "Sad Philomel her song in tears doth steep." And Mr. Philips, by a poetical creation, hath raised up finer beds of flowers than the most industrious gardener; his roses, lilies, and daffodils blow in the same season.

But the better to discover the merits of our two contemporary pastoral writers, I shall endeavor to draw a parallel of them by setting several of their particular thoughts in the same light, whereby it will be obvious how much Philips hath the advantage. With what simplicity he introduces two shepherds singing alternately:

> *Hobb.*   Come, Rosalind, O come, for without thee
> What pleasure can the country have for me:
> Come, Rosalind, O come; my brinded kine,
> My snowy sheep, my farm, and all is thine.
> *Lanq.*   Come Rosalind, O come; here shady bowers,
> Here are cool fountains, and here springing flowers.
> Come, Rosalind; here ever let us stay,
> And sweetly waste our live-long time away.

4. Famiano Strada (1572–1649), Italian rhetorician and poet.

Our other pastoral writer, in expressing the same thought, deviates into downright poetry:

> *Streph.* In spring the fields, in autumn hills I love,
> At morn the plains, at noon the shady grove,
> But Delia always; forced from Delia's sight,
> Nor plains at morn, nor groves at noon delight.
>
> *Daph.* Sylvia's like autumn ripe, yet mild as May,
> More bright than noon, yet fresh as early day;
> Even spring displeases, when she shines not here.
> But blest with her, 'tis spring throughout the year.

In the first of these authors, two shepherds thus innocently describe the behavior of their mistresses:

> *Hobb.* As Marian bathed, by chance I passed by,
> She blushed, and at me cast a side-long eye;
> Then swift beneath the crystal wave she tried
> Her beauteous form, but all in vain, to hide.
>
> *Lanq.* As I to cool me bathed one sultry day,
> Fond Lydia lurking in the sedges lay.
> The wanton laughed, and seemed in haste to fly;
> Yet often stopped, and often turned her eye.

The other modern (who it must be confessed hath a knack of versifying) hath it as follows:

> *Streph.* Me gentle Delia beckons from the plain,
> Then, hid in shades, eludes her eager swain;
> But feigns a laugh, to see me search around,
> And by that laugh the willing fair is found.
>
> *Daph.* The sprightly Sylvia trips along the green,
> She runs, but hopes she does not run unseen;
> While a kind glance at her pursuer flies,
> How much at variance are her feet and eyes!

There is nothing the writers of this kind of poetry are fonder of than descriptions of pastoral presents. Philips says thus of a sheep-hook:

> Of seasoned elm, where studs of brass appear,
> To speak the giver's name, the month and year.
> The hook of polished steel, the handle turned,
> And richly by the graver's skill adorned.

The other of a bowl embossed with figures:

> Where wanton ivy twines,
> And swelling clusters bend the curling vines;
> Four figures rising from the work appear,
> The various seasons of the rolling year;
> And what is that which binds the radiant sky,
> Where twelve bright signs in beauteous order lie?

The simplicity of the swain in this place who forgets the name of the Zodiac is no ill imitation of Virgil; but how much more plainly and unaffectedly would Philips have dressed this thought in his Doric?

> And what that hight, which girds the welkin sheen,
> Where twelve gay signs in meet array are seen.

If the reader would indulge his curiosity any farther in the comparison of particulars, he may read the first pastoral of Philips with the second of his contemporary, and the fourth and sixth of the former with the fourth and first of the latter, where several parallel places will occur to everyone.

Having now shown some parts in which these two writers may be compared, it is a justice I owe to Mr. Philips to discover those in which no man can compare with him. First, that *beautiful rusticity,* of which I shall only produce two instances, out of a hundred not yet quoted:

> O woeful day! O day of woe, quoth he,
> And woeful I, who live the day to see!

That simplicity of diction, the melancholy flowing of the numbers, the solemnity of the sound, and the easy turn of the words in this *dirge* (to make use of our author's expression) are extremely elegant.

In another of his pastorals, a shepherd utters a dirge not much inferior to the former, in the following lines:

> Ah me the while! ah me! the luckless day!
> Ah luckless lad! the rather might I say;
> Ah silly I! more silly than my sheep,
> Which on the flowery plains I once did keep.

How he still charms the ear with these artful repetitions of the epithets, and how significant is the last verse! I defy the most common reader to repeat them without feeling some motions of compassion.

In the next place I shall rank his proverbs, in which I formerly observed he excels. For example:

> A rolling stone is ever bare of moss;
> And, to their cost, green years old proverbs cross.

> He that late lies down as late will rise,
> And, sluggard-like, till noon-day snoring lies.

> Against ill luck all cunning foresight fails;
> Whether we sleep or wake it nought avails.

> Nor fear, from upright sentence, wrong.

Lastly, his elegant dialect, which alone might prove him the eldest born of Spenser and our only true Arcadian; I should think it proper for the several writers of pastoral to confine themselves to their several counties. Spenser seems to have been of this opinion; for he hath laid the scene of one of his pastorals in Wales, where, with all the simplicity natural to that part of our island, one shepherd bids the other good-morrow in an unusual and elegant manner:

> Diggon Davy, I bid hur God-day;
> Or Diggon hur is, or I mis-say.

Diggon answers,

> Hur was hur while it was day-light;
> But now hur is a most wretched wight, etc.[5]

But the most beautiful example of this kind that I ever met with is in a very valuable piece which I chanced to find among some old manuscripts, entitled "A Pastoral Ballad," which I think for its nature and simplicity may (notwithstanding the modesty of the title) be allowed a perfect pastoral. It is composed in the Somersetshire dialect, and the names such as are proper to the country people. It may be observed, as a further beauty of this pastoral, the words *nymph, dryad, naiad, fawn, Cupid,* or *satyr* are not once mentioned through the whole. I shall make

5. *Shepherd's Calendar,* "September," 1–4.

no apology for inserting some few lines of this excellent piece.
Cicily breaks thus into the subject, as she is going a-milking:

> *Cicily.* Rager go vetch tha kee,[6] or else tha zun
> Will quite be go, be vore c'have half a don.
> *Roger.* Thou shouldst not ax ma tweece, but I've a be
> To dreave our bull to bull tha parson's kee.

It is to be observed that this whole dialogue is formed upon the
passion of jealousy; and his mentioning the parson's kine naturally revives the jealousy of the shepherdess Cicily, which she
expresses as follows:

> *Cicily.* Ah Rager, Rager, chez was zore avraid
> Ween in yond vield you kissed tha parson's maid;
> Is this the love that once to me you zed,
> When from tha wake thou brought'st me gingerbread?
> *Roger.* Cicily, thou charg'st me false,—I'll zwear to thee,
> Tha parson's maid is still a maid for me.

In which answer of his are expressed at once that spirit of religion
and that innocence of the Golden Age so necessary to be observed
by all writers of pastoral.

At the conclusion of this piece, the author reconciles the lovers
and ends the eclogue the most simply in the world:

> So Rager parted vor to vetch the kee,
> And vor her bucket in went Cicily.

I am loath to show my fondness for antiquity so far as to prefer
this ancient British author to our present English writers of
pastoral; but I cannot avoid making this obvious remark, that
both Spenser and Philips have hit into the same road with this
old West Country bard of ours.

After all that hath been said, I hope none can think it any
injustice to Mr. Pope that I forebore to mention him as a pastoral
writer, since upon the whole he is of the same class with Moschus
and Bion, whom we have excluded that rank, and of whose
eclogues, as well as some of Virgil's, it may be said that, according
to the description we have given of this sort of poetry, they are
by no means pastorals, but something better.

6. That is, the kine or cows [Pope].

CRITICISM OF EPIC

Preface to the Translation of the *Iliad* (1715)

Homer is universally allowed to have had the greatest invention of any writer whatever. The praise of judgment Virgil has justly contested with him, and others may have their pretensions as to particular excellencies; but his invention remains yet unrivaled. Nor is it a wonder if he has ever been acknowledged the greatest of poets, who most excelled in that which is the very foundation of poetry. It is the invention that in different degrees distinguishes all great geniuses; the utmost stretch of human study, learning, and industry, which masters everything besides, can never attain to this. It furnishes Art with all her materials, and without it judgment itself can at best but *steal wisely*. For Art is only like a prudent steward that lives on managing the riches of Nature. Whatever praises may be given to works of judgment, there is not even a single beauty in them but is owing to the invention; as in the most regular gardens, however Art may carry the greatest appearance, there is not a plant or flower but is the gift of Nature. The first can only reduce the beauties of the latter into a more obvious figure, which the common eye may better take in and is therefore more entertained with. And perhaps the reason why most critics are inclined to prefer a judicious and methodical genius to a great and fruitful one is because they find it easier for themselves to pursue their observations through an uniform and bounded walk of Art than to comprehend the vast and various extent of Nature.

Our author's work is a wild paradise, where, if we cannot see all the beauties so distinctly as in an ordered garden, it is only because the number of them is infinitely greater. 'Tis like a copious nursery which contains the seeds and first productions of every kind, out of which those who followed him have but selected some particular plants, each according to his fancy, to cultivate and beautify. If some things are too luxuriant, it is

108   LITERARY CRITICISM OF POPE

owing to the richness of the soil; and if others are not arrived to
perfection or maturity, it is only because they are overrun and
oppressed by those of a stronger nature.

It is to the strength of this amazing invention we are to attribute that unequaled fire and rapture which is so forcible in Homer
that no man of a true poetical spirit is master of himself while
he reads him. What he writes is of the most animated nature
imaginable; everything moves, everything lives and is put in
action. If a council be called or a battle fought, you are not coldly
informed of what was said or done as from a third person; the
reader is hurried out of himself by the force of the poet's imagination and turns in one place to a hearer, in another to a spectator.
The course of his verses resembles that of the army he describes,
Οἱ δ᾽ ἄρ᾽ ἴσαν ὡς εἴ τε πυρὶ χθὼν πᾶσα νέμοιτο. They pour along
like a fire that sweeps the whole earth before it."[1] 'Tis however
remarkable that his fancy, which is everywhere vigorous, is not
discovered immediately at the beginning of his poem in its fullest
splendor; it grows in the progress both upon himself and others,
and becomes on fire like a chariot-wheel, by its own rapidity.
Exact disposition, just thought, correct elocution, polished numbers may have been found in a thousand; but this poetical *fire*,
this *vivida vis animi*,[2] in a very few. Even in works where all
those are imperfect or neglected, this can overpower criticism
and make us admire even while we disapprove. Nay, where this
appears, though attended with absurdities, it brightens all the
rubbish about it, till we see nothing but its own splendor. This
fire is discerned in Virgil, but discerned as through a glass, reflected, and more shining than warm, but everywhere equal and
constant. In Lucan and Statius it bursts out in sudden, short,
and interrupted flashes; in Milton it glows like a furnace kept
up to an uncommon fierceness by the force of art; in Shakespeare
it strikes before we are aware, like an accidental fire from Heaven;
but in Homer, and in him only, it burns everywhere clearly and
everywhere irresistibly.

I shall here endeavor to show how this vast invention exerts

1. *Iliad*, II, 780.
2. "Active power of the mind."

itself in a manner superior to that of any poet, through all the main constituent parts of his work, as it is the great and peculiar characteristic which distinguishes him from all other authors. This strong and ruling faculty was like a powerful planet, which in the violence of its own course drew all things within its vortex. It seemed not enough to have taken in the whole circle of arts and the whole compass of Nature; all the inward passions and affections of mankind to supply his[3] characters and all the outward forms and images of things for his descriptions; but wanting yet an ampler sphere to expatiate in, he opened a new and boundless walk for his imagination and created a world for himself in the invention of *fable*. That which Aristotle calls the "soul of poetry"[4] was first breathed into it by Homer. I shall begin with considering him in this part, as it is naturally the first, and I speak of it both as it means the design of a poem and as it is taken for fiction.

Fable may be divided into the probable, the allegorical, and the marvelous. The probable fable is the recital of such actions as, though they did not happen, yet might, in the common course of Nature, or of such as, though they did, become fables by the additional episodes and manner of telling them. Of this sort is the main story of an epic poem, the return of Ulysses, the settlement of the Trojans in Italy, or the like. That of the *Iliad* is the anger of Achilles, the most short and single subject that ever was chosen by any poet. Yet this he has supplied with a vaster variety of incidents and events, and crowded with a greater number of councils, speeches, battles, and episodes of all kinds than are to be found even in those poems whose schemes are of the utmost latitude and irregularity. The action is hurried on with the most vehement spirit, and its whole duration employs not so much as fifty days. Virgil, for want of so warm a genius, aided himself by taking in a more extensive subject, as well as a greater length of time, and contracting the design of both Homer's poems into one which is yet but a fourth part as large as his. The other epic poets have used the same practice, but generally carried it so far

3. "This" in the first edition.
4. *Poetics*, VI.

as to superinduce a multiplicity of fables, destroy the unity of action, and lose their readers in an unreasonable length of time. Nor is it only in the main design that they have been unable to add to his invention, but they have followed him in every episode and part of story. If he has given a regular catalogue of an army, they all draw up their forces in the same order. If he has funeral games for Patroclus, Virgil has the same for Anchises, and Statius (rather than omit them) destroys the unity of his action for those of Archemorus. If Ulysses visit the Shades, the Aeneas of Virgil and Scipio of Silius are sent after him. If he be detained from his return by the allurements of Calypso, so is Aeneas by Dido and Rinaldo by Armida. If Achilles be absent from the army on the score of a quarrel through half the poem, Rinaldo must absent himself just as long on the like account. If he gives his hero a suit of celestial armor, Virgil and Tasso make the same present to theirs. Virgil has not only observed this close imitation of Homer but, where he had not led the way, supplied the want from other Greek authors. Thus the story of Sinon and the taking of Troy was copied (says Macrobius)[5] almost word for word from Pisander, as the loves of Dido and Aeneas are taken from those of Medea and Jason in Apollonius, and several others in the same manner.

To proceed to the allegorical fable: if we reflect upon those innumerable knowledges, those secrets of Nature and physical philosophy which Homer is generally supposed to have wrapped up in his allegories, what a new and ample scene of wonder may this consideration afford us? How fertile will that imagination appear which was able to clothe all the properties of elements, the qualifications of the mind, the virtues and vices, in forms and persons, and to introduce them into actions agreeable to the nature of the things they shadowed? This is a field in which no succeeding poets could dispute with Homer; and whatever commendations have been allowed them on this head are by no means for their invention in having enlarged his circle but for their judgment in having contracted it. For when the mode of learning changed in following ages and science was delivered in

5. *Saturnalia*, V, ii.

a plainer manner, it then became as reasonable in the more modern poets to lay it aside as it was in Homer to make use of it. And perhaps it was no unhappy circumstance for Virgil that there was not in his time that demand upon him of so great an invention as might be capable of furnishing all those allegorical parts of a poem.

The marvellous fable includes whatever is supernatural and especially the machines of the gods. If Homer was not the first who introduced the deities (as Herodotus imagines) into the religion of Greece, he seems the first who brought them into a system of machinery for poetry, and such an one as makes its greatest importance and dignity. For we find those authors who have been offended at the literal notion of the gods constantly laying their accusation against Homer as the undoubted inventor of them. But whatever cause there might be to blame his machines in a philosophical or religious view, they are so perfect in the poetic that mankind have been ever since contented to follow them. None have been able to enlarge the sphere of poetry beyond the limits he has set; every attempt of this nature has proved unsuccessful; and after all the various changes of times and religions, his gods continue to this day the gods of poetry.

We come now to the characters of his persons, and here we shall find no author has ever drawn so many with so visible and surprising a variety or given us such lively and affecting impressions of them. Every one has something so singularly his own that no painter could have distinguished them more by their features than the poet has by their manners. Nothing can be more exact than the distinctions he has observed in the different degrees of virtues and vices. The single quality of courage is wonderfully diversified in the several characters of the *Iliad*. That of Achilles is furious and intractable; that of Diomede forward, yet listening to advice and subject to command; we see in Ajax an heavy and self-considering valor, in Hector an active and vigilant one; the courage of Agamemnon is inspirited by love of empire and ambition, that of Menelaus mixed with softness and tenderness for his people; we find in Idomeneus a plain, direct soldier, in Sarpedon a gallant and generous one. Nor is this judicious and astonishing diversity to be found only in the principal quality which constitutes the main of each character, but even in the under-parts of it, to which he takes care to give a tincture of that principal one. For example, the main characters of Ulysses and Nestor consist in wisdom, and they are distinct in this; the wisdom of one is artificial and various, of the other natural, open, and regular. But they have, besides, characters of courage; and this quality also takes a different turn in each from the difference of his prudence, for one in the war depends still upon caution, the other upon experience. It would be endless to produce instances of these kinds. The characters of Virgil are far from striking us in this open manner; they lie in a great degree hidden and undistinguished, and, where they are marked most evidently, affect us not in proportion to those of Homer. His characters of valor are much alike; even that of Turnus seems no way peculiar but as it is in a superior degree; and we see nothing that differences the courage of Mnestheus from that of Sergesthus, Cloanthus, or the rest. In like manner it may be remarked of Statius's heroes that an air of impetuosity runs through them all; the same horrid and savage courage appears in his Capaneus, Tydeus, Hippomedon, etc. They have a parity of character which makes them seem brothers of one family. I believe when the reader is led into this track of reflection, if he will pursue it through the epic and tragic writers, he will be convinced how infinitely superior in this point the invention of Homer was to that of all others.

The *speeches* are to be considered as they flow from the characters, being perfect or defective as they agree or disagree with the manners of those who utter them. As there is more variety of characters in the *Iliad*, so there is of speeches, than in any other poem. "Everything in it has manners" (as Aristotle expresses it);[6] that is, everything is acted or spoken. It is hardly credible in a work of such length how small a number of lines are employed in narration. In Virgil the dramatic part is less in proportion to the narrative; and the speeches often consist of general reflections or thoughts which might be equally just in any person's mouth

6. *Poetics,* XXIV.

upon the same occasion. As many of his persons have no apparent characters, so many of his speeches escape being applied and judged by the rule of propriety. We oftener think of the author himself when we read Virgil than when we are engaged in Homer. All which are the effects of a colder invention that interests us less in the action described: Homer makes us hearers, and Virgil leaves us readers.

If in the next place we take a view of the *sentiments*, the same presiding faculty is eminent in the sublimity and spirit of his thoughts. Longinus has given his opinion that it was in this part Homer principally excelled. What were alone sufficient to prove the grandeur and excellence of his sentiments in general is that they have so remarkable a parity with those of the Scripture; Duport, in his *Gnomologia Homerica*, has collected innumerable instances of this sort.[7] And it is with justice an excellent modern writer allows that if Virgil has not so many thoughts that are low and vulgar, he has not so many that are sublime and noble, and that the Roman author seldom rises into very astonishing sentiments where he is not fired by the *Iliad*.[8]

If we observe his *descriptions, images*, and *similes*, we shall find the invention still predominant. To what else can we ascribe that vast comprehension of images of every sort, where we see each circumstance and individual of Nature summoned together by the extent and fecundity of his imagination, to which all things, in their various views, presented themselves in an instant and had their impressions taken off to perfection at a heat? Nay, he not only gives us the full prospects of things but several unexpected peculiarities and side-views, unobserved by any painter but Homer. Nothing is so surprising as the descriptions of his battles, which take up no less than half the *Iliad* and are supplied with so vast a variety of incidents that no one bears a likeness to another, such different kinds of deaths that no two heroes are wounded in the same manner, and such a profusion of noble ideas that every battle rises above the last in greatness, horror, and confusion. It is certain there is not near that number of

7. James Duport, *Homeri Gnomologia* (1660).
8. Addison, in *Spectator* No. 279.

images and descriptions in any epic poet, though everyone has assisted himself with a great quantity out of him; and it is evident of Virgil, especially, that he has scarce any comparisons which are not drawn from his master.

If we descend from hence to the *expression*, we see the bright imagination of Homer shining out in the most enlivened forms of it. We acknowledge him the father of poetical diction, the first who taught that language of the gods to men. His expression is like the coloring of some great masters, which discovers itself to be laid on boldly and executed with rapidity. It is indeed the strongest and most glowing imaginable, and touched with the greatest spirit. Aristotle had reason to say he was the only poet who had found out "living words";[9] there are in him more daring figures and metaphors than in any good author whatever. An arrow is "impatient" to be on the wing, a weapon "thirsts" to drink the blood of an enemy, and the like. Yet his expression is never too big for the sense, but justly great in proportion to it; 'tis the sentiment that swells and fills out the diction, which rises with it and forms itself about it. For in the same degree that a thought is warmer, an expression will be brighter; and as that is more strong, this will become more perspicuous, like glass in the furnace, which grows to a greater magnitude and refines to a greater clearness only as the breath within is more powerful and the heat more intense.

To throw his language more out of prose, Homer seems to have affected the compound epithets. This was a sort of composition peculiarly proper to poetry, not only as it heightened the diction, but as it assisted and filled the numbers with greater sound and pomp, and likewise conduced in some measure to thicken the images. On this last consideration I cannot but attribute these to the fruitfulness of his invention, since (as he has managed them) they are a sort of supernumerary pictures of the persons or things they are joined to. We see the motion of Hector's plumes in the epithet κορυθαιόλος, the landscape of Mount Neritus in that of εἰνοσίφυλλος,[10] and so of others; which particu-

---

9. *Rhetoric*, III, xi.
10. "With the glancing helm"; "with quivering foliage."

lar images could not have been insisted upon so long as to express
them in a description (though but of a single line) without diverting the reader too much from the principal action or figure. As a
metaphor is a short simile, one of these epithets is a short description.

Lastly, if we consider his *versification*, we shall be sensible
what a share of praise is due to his invention in that also. He was
not satisfied with his language as he found it settled in any one
part of Greece, but searched through its differing dialects with
this particular view, to beautify and perfect his numbers; he considered these as they had a greater mixture of vowels or consonants and accordingly employed them as the verse required either
a greater smoothness or strength. What he most affected was the
Ionic, which has a peculiar sweetness from its never using contractions and from its custom of resolving the diphthongs into
two syllables, so as to make the words open themselves with a
more spreading and sonorous fluency. With this he mingled the
Attic contractions, the broader Doric, and the feebler Aeolic,
which often rejects its aspirate or takes off its accent, and com-
pleted this variety by altering some letters with the license of
poetry. Thus his measures, instead of being fetters to his sense,
were always in readiness to run along with the warmth of his
rapture and even to give a farther representation of his notions
in the correspondence of their sounds to what they signified. Out
of all these he has derived that harmony which makes us confess
he had not only the richest head but the finest ear in the world.
This is so great a truth that whoever will but consult the tune of
his verses even without understanding them (with the same sort
of diligence as we daily see practiced in the case of Italian operas)
will find more sweetness, variety, and majesty of sound than in
any other language or poetry. The beauty of his numbers is
allowed by the critics to be copied but faintly by Virgil himself,
though they are so just to ascribe it to the nature of the Latin
tongue. Indeed the Greek has some advantages both from the
natural sound of its words and the turn and cadence of its verse,
which agree with the genius of no other language. Virgil was very
sensible of this and used the utmost diligence in working up a

more intractable language to whatsoever graces it was capable of, and in particular never failed to bring the sound of his line to a beautiful agreement with its sense. If the Grecian poet has not been so frequently celebrated on this account as the Roman, the only reason is that fewer critics have understood one language than the other. Dionysius of Halicarnassus has pointed out many of our author's beauties in this kind in his treatise of the *Composition of Words*, and others will be taken notice of in the course of the notes. It suffices at present to observe of his numbers that they flow with so much ease as to make one imagine Homer had no other care than to transcribe as fast as the Muses dictated, and at the same time with so much force and inspiriting vigor that they awaken and raise us like the sound of a trumpet. They roll along as a plentiful river, always in motion and always full, while we are borne away by a tide of verse the most rapid and yet the most smooth imaginable.

Thus, on whatever side we contemplate Homer, what principally strikes us is his *invention*. It is that which forms the character of each part of his work; and accordingly we find it to have made his fable more extensive and copious than any other, his manners more lively and strongly marked, his speeches more affecting and transported, his sentiments more warm and sublime, his images and descriptions more full and animated, his expression more raised and daring, and his numbers more rapid and various. I hope in what has been said of Virgil with regard to any of these heads, I have no way derogated from his character. Nothing is more absurd or endless than the common method of comparing eminent writers by an opposition of particular passages in them and forming a judgment from thence of their merit upon the whole. We ought to have a certain knowledge of the principal character and distinguishing excellence of each; it is in *that* we are to consider him, and in proportion to his degree in *that* we are to admire him. No author or man ever excelled all the world in more than one faculty, and as Homer has done this in invention, Virgil has in judgment. Not that we are to think Homer wanted judgment because Virgil had it in a more eminent degree, or that Virgil wanted invention because Homer possessed a larger share of it: each of these great authors had more of both than perhaps any man besides, and are only said to have less in comparison with one another. Homer was the greater genius, Virgil the better artist. In one we most admire the man, in the other the work. Homer hurries and transports us with a commanding impetuosity, Virgil leads us with an attractive majesty. Homer scatters with a generous profusion, Virgil bestows with a careful magnificence. Homer, like the Nile, pours out his riches with a sudden overflow; Virgil, like a river in its banks, with a gentle and constant stream. When we behold their battles, methinks the two poets resemble the heroes they celebrate: Homer, boundless and irresistible as Achilles, bears all before him, and shines more and more as the tumult increases; Virgil, calmly daring like Aeneas, appears undisturbed in the midst of the action, disposes all about him, and conquers with tranquillity. And when we look upon their machines, Homer seems like his own Jupiter in his terrors, shaking Olympus, scattering the lightnings, and firing the Heavens; Virgil, like the same power in his benevolence, counselling with the gods, laying plans for empires, and regularly ordering his whole creation.

But, after all, it is with great parts as with great virtues, they naturally border on some imperfection; and it is often hard to distinguish exactly where the virtue ends or the fault begins. As prudence may sometimes sink to suspicion, so may a great judgment decline to coldness; and as magnanimity may run up to profusion or extravagance, so may a great invention to redundancy or wildness. If we look upon Homer in this view, we shall perceive the chief objections against him to proceed from so noble a cause as the excess of this faculty.

Among these we may reckon some of his marvelous fictions, upon which so much criticism has been spent as surpassing all the bounds of probability. Perhaps it may be with great and superior souls as with gigantic bodies, which, exerting themselves with unusual strength, exceed what is commonly thought the due proportion of parts to become miracles in the whole and, like the old heroes of that make, commit something near extravagance amidst a series of glorious and inimitable performances. Thus

Homer has his speaking horses, and Virgil has myrtles distilling blood, without so much as contriving the easy intervention of a deity to save the probability.

It is owing to the same vast invention that his similes have been thought too exuberant and full of circumstances. The force of this faculty is seen in nothing more than its inability to confine itself to that single circumstance upon which the comparison is grounded. It runs out into embellishments of additional images, which, however, are so managed as not to overpower the main one. His similes are like pictures where the principal figure has not only its proportion given agreeable to the original but is also set off with occasional ornaments and prospects. The same will account for his manner of heaping a number of comparisons together in one breath when his fancy suggested to him at once so many various and correspondent images. The reader will easily extend this observation to more objections of the same kind.

If there are others which seem rather to charge him with a defect or narrowness of genius than an excess of it, those seeming defects will be found upon examination to proceed wholly from the nature of the times he lived in. Such are his grosser representations of the gods and the vicious and imperfect manners of his heroes, which will be treated of in the following essay.[11] But I must here speak a word of the latter, as it is a point generally carried into extremes both by the censurers and defenders of Homer. It must be a strange partiality to antiquity to think with Madame Dacier, "that those times and manners are so much the more excellent as they are more contrary to ours."[12] Who can be so prejudiced in their favor as to magnify the felicity of those ages, when a spirit of revenge and cruelty reigned through the world, when no mercy was shown but for the sake of lucre, when the greatest princes were put to the sword and their wives and

11. See the articles of theology and morality in the third part of the Essay [Pope]. The "Essay on the Life, Writing, and Learning of Homer" prefixed to Pope's translation is by Thomas Parnell.

12. Preface to her *Homer* [Pope]. In the following pages Pope touches on the Ancient-Modern controversy in France, in which Madame Dacier defended Homer against the strictures of La Motte.

daughters made slaves and concubines? On the other side, I would not be so delicate as those modern critics who are shocked at the "servile offices" and "mean employments" in which we sometimes see the heroes of Homer engaged. There is a pleasure in taking a view of that simplicity in opposition to the luxury of succeeding ages, in beholding monarchs without their guards, princes tending their flocks, and princesses drawing water from the springs. When we read Homer, we ought to reflect that we are reading the most ancient author in the heathen world; and those who consider him in this light will double their pleasure in the perusal of him. Let them think they are growing acquainted with nations and people that are now no more; that they are stepping almost three thousand years backward into the remotest antiquity and entertaining themselves with a clear and surprising vision of things nowhere else to be found, and the only authentic picture of that ancient world. By this means alone their greatest obstacles will vanish; and what usually creates their dislike will become a satisfaction.

This consideration may farther serve to answer for the constant use of the same epithets to his gods and heroes, such as the "far-darting Phoebus," the "blue-eyed Pallas," the "swift-footed Achilles," etc., which some have censured as impertinent and tediously repeated. Those of the gods depended upon the powers and offices then believed to belong to them, and had contracted a weight and veneration from the rites and solemn devotions in which they were used. They were a sort of attributes that it was a matter of religion to salute them with on all occasions and an irreverence to omit. As for the epithets of great men, M. Boileau is of opinion that they were in the nature of surnames, and repeated as such; for the Greeks, having no names derived from their fathers, were obliged when they mentioned anyone to add some other distinction, either naming his parents expressly, or his place of birth, profession, or the like, as "Alexander son of Philip," "Herodotus of Halicarnassus," "Diogenes the Cynic," etc. Homer, therefore, complying with the custom of his country, used such distinctive additions as better agreed with poetry. And indeed we have something parallel to these in modern times, such as the names of "Harold Harefoot," "Edmund Ironside," "Edward Longshanks," "Edward the Black Prince," etc. If yet this be thought to account better for the propriety than for the repetition, I shall add a farther conjecture. Hesiod, dividing the world into its ages, has placed a fourth age between the brazen and the iron one, of "heroes distinct from other men, a divine race, who fought at Thebes and Troy, are called demi-gods, and live by the care of Jupiter in the Islands of the Blessed."[13] Now among the divine honors which were paid them, they might have this also in common with the gods, not to be mentioned without the solemnity of an epithet, and such as might be acceptable to them by its celebrating their families, actions, or qualities.

What other cavils have been raised against Homer are such as hardly deserve a reply, but will yet be taken notice of as they occur in the course of the work. Many have been occasioned by an injudicious endeavor to exalt Virgil, which is much the same as if one should think to raise[14] the superstructure by undermining the foundation. One would imagine by the whole course of their parallels that these critics never so much as heard of Homer's having written first, a consideration which whoever compares these two poets ought to have always in his eye. Some accuse him for the same things which they overlook or praise in the other, as when they prefer the fable and moral of the *Aeneis* to those of the *Iliad*, for the same reasons which might set the *Odysses* above the *Aeneis*: as that the hero is a wiser man and the action of the one more beneficial to his country than that of the other. Or else they blame him for not doing what he never designed, as because Achilles is not as good and perfect a prince as Aeneas, when the very moral of his poem required a contrary character. It is thus that Rapin judges in his comparison of Homer and Virgil.[15] Others select those particular passages of Homer which are not so labored as some that Virgil drew out of them; this is the whole management of Scaliger in his *Poetices*.

13. Hesiod, *lib*. I, ver. 155, etc. [Pope].
14. "Praise" in the first edition.
15. René Rapin, *Observations on the Poems of Homer and Virgil* (English tr. 1672).

Others quarrel with what they take for low and mean expressions, sometimes through a false delicacy and refinement, oftener from an ignorance of the graces of the original, and then triumph in the awkwardness of their own translations. This is the conduct of Perrault in his *Parallels*.[16] Lastly, there are others who, pretending to a fairer proceeding, distinguish between the personal merit of Homer and that of his work; but when they come to assign the causes of the great reputation of the *Iliad*, they found it upon the ignorance of his times and the prejudice of those that followed. And, in pursuance of this principle, they make those accidents (such as the contention of the cities, etc.) to be the causes of his fame which were in reality the consequences of his merit. The same might as well be said of Virgil or any great author whose general character will infallibly raise many casual additions to their reputation. This is the method of M. de la Motte,[17] who yet confesses upon the whole that in whatever age Homer had lived he must have been the greatest poet of his nation and that he may be said in this sense to be the master even of those who surpassed him.

In all these objections we see nothing that contradicts his title to the honor of the chief invention, and as long as this (which is indeed the characteristic of poetry itself) remains unequaled by his followers, he still continues superior to them. A cooler judgment may commit fewer faults and be more approved in the eyes of one sort of critics, but that warmth of fancy will carry the loudest and most universal applauses which holds the heart of a reader under the strongest enchantment. Homer not only appears the inventor of poetry, but excels all the inventors of other arts in this, that he has swallowed up the honor of those who succeeded him. What he has done admitted no increase, it only left room for contraction or regulation. He showed all the stretch of fancy at once; and if he has failed in some of his flights, it was but because he attempted everything. A work of this kind seems like a mighty tree which rises from the most vigorous seed, is improved with industry, flourishes, and produces the finest fruit;

16. Charles Perrault, *Parallèle des Anciens et des Modernes* (1686–1696).
17. Antoine Houdar de la Motte, *Discours sur Homère* (1714).

Nature and Art have conspired to raise it; pleasure and profit joined to make it valuable; and they who find the justest faults have only said that a few branches (which run luxuriant through a richness of Nature) might be lopped into form to give it a more regular appearance.

Having now spoken of the beauties and defects of the original, it remains to treat of the translation, with the same view to the chief characteristic. As far as that is seen in the main parts of the poem, such as the fable, manners, and sentiments, no translator can prejudice it but by willful omissions or contractions. As it also breaks out in every particular image, description, and simile, whoever lessens or too much softens those takes off from this chief character. It is the first grand duty of an interpreter to give his author entire and unmaimed; and for the rest, the diction and versification only are his proper province, since these must be his own, but the others he is to take as he finds them.

It should then be considered what methods may afford some equivalent in our language for the graces of these in the Greek. It is certain no literal translation can be just to an excellent original in a superior language, but it is a great mistake to imagine (as many have done) that a rash paraphrase can make amends for this general defect, which is no less in danger to lose the spirit of an Ancient by deviating into the modern manners of expression. If there be sometimes a darkness, there is often a light in antiquity, which nothing better preserves than a version almost literal. I know no liberties one ought to take but those which are necessary for transfusing the spirit of the original and supporting the poetical style of the translation; and I will venture to say there have not been more men misled in former times by a servile dull adherence to the letter than have been deluded in ours by a chimerical insolent hope of raising and improving their author. It is not to be doubted that the *fire* of the poem is what a translator should principally regard, as it is most likely to expire in his managing. However, it is his safest way to be content with preserving this to his utmost in the whole, without endeavoring to be more than he finds his author is in any particular place. 'Tis a great secret in writing to know when to be plain, and when poetical and figurative; and it is what Homer will teach us if we will but follow modestly in his footsteps. Where his diction is bold and lofty, let us raise ours as high as we can; but where his is plain and humble, we ought not to be deterred from imitating him by the fear of incurring the censure of a mere English critic. Nothing that belongs to Homer seems to have been more commonly mistaken than the just pitch of his style, some of his translators having swelled into fustian in a proud confidence of the sublime, others sunk into flatness in a cold and timorous notion of simplicity. Methinks I see these different followers of Homer, some sweating and straining after him by violent leaps and bounds (the certain signs of false mettle), others slowly and servilely creeping in his train, while the poet himself is all the time proceeding with an unaffected and equal majesty before them. However, of the two extremes one could sooner pardon frenzy than frigidity; no author is to be envied for such commendations as he may gain by that character of style which his friends must agree together to call simplicity and the rest of the world will call dullness. There is a graceful and dignified simplicity, as well as a bald and sordid one, which differ as much from each other as the air of a plain man from that of a sloven. 'Tis one thing to be tricked up, and another not to be dressed at all. Simplicity is the mean between ostentation and rusticity.

This pure and noble simplicity is nowhere in such perfection as in the Scripture and our author. One may affirm with all respect to the inspired writings that the Divine Spirit made use of no other words but what were intelligible and common to men at that time and in that part of the world; and as Homer is the author nearest to those, his style must of course bear a greater resemblance to the Sacred Books than that of any other writer. This consideration (together with what has been observed of the parity of some of his thoughts) may, methinks, induce a translator, on the one hand, to give into several of those general phrases and manners of expression which have attained a veneration even in our language from their use in the Old Testament, as, on the other, to avoid those which have been appropriated to the divinity and in a manner consigned to mystery and religion.

For a farther preservation of this air of simplicity, a particular care should be taken to express with all plainness those moral sentences and proverbial speeches which are so numerous in this poet. They have something venerable and, as I may say, oracular in that unadorned gravity and shortness with which they are delivered, a grace which would be utterly lost by endeavoring to give them what we call a more ingenious (that is, a more modern) turn in the paraphrase.

Perhaps the mixture of some Graecisms and old words after the manner of Milton, if done without too much affectation, might not have an ill effect in a version of this particular work, which most of any other seems to require a venerable antique cast. But certainly the use of modern terms of war and government, such as "platoon," "campaign," "junto," or the like, (which some of his translators have fallen into) cannot be allowable, those only excepted without which it is impossible to treat the subjects in any living language.

There are two peculiarities in Homer's diction that are a sort of marks or moles, by which every common eye distinguishes him at first sight. Those who are not his greatest admirers look upon them as defects, and those who are seem pleased with them as beauties. I speak of his compound epithets and of his repetitions. Many of the former cannot be done literally into English without destroying the purity of our language. I believe such should be retained as slide easily of themselves into an English compound without violence to the ear or to the received rules of composition, as well as those which have received a sanction from the authority of our best poets and are become familiar through their use of them, such as the "cloud-compelling Jove," etc. As for the rest, whenever any can be as fully and significantly expressed in a single word as in a compounded one, the course to be taken is obvious. Some that cannot be so turned as to preserve their full image by one or two words may have justice done them by circumlocution, as the epithet εἰνοσίφυλλος to a mountain would appear little or ridiculous translated literally "leaf-shaking," but affords a majestic idea in the periphrasis: "the lofty mountain shakes his waving woods." Others that admit of differing significations may receive an advantage by a judicious variation according to the occasions on which they are introduced. For example, the epithet of Apollo, ἑκηβόλος, or "far-shooting," is capable of two explications, one literal in respect of the darts and bow, the ensigns of that god, the other allegorical with regard to the rays of the sun; therefore in such places where Apollo is represented as a god in person, I would use the former interpretation, and where the effects of the sun are described, I would make choice of the latter. Upon the whole, it will be necessary to avoid that perpetual repetition of the same epithets which we find in Homer and which, though it might be accommodated (as has been already shown) to the ear of those times, is by no means so to ours. But one may wait for opportunities of placing them where they derive an additional beauty from the occasions on which they are employed, and in doing this properly a translator may at once show his fancy and his judgment.

As for Homer's repetitions, we may divide them into three sorts: of whole narrations and speeches, of single sentences, and of one verse or hemistich. I hope it is not impossible to have such a regard to these as neither to lose so known a mark of the author on the one hand, nor to offend the reader too much on the other. The repetition is not ungraceful in those speeches where the dignity of the speaker renders it a sort of insolence to alter his words, as in the messages from gods to men, or from higher powers to inferiors in concerns of state, or where the ceremonial of religion seems to require it, in the solemn forms of prayers, oaths, or the like. In other cases, I believe the best rule is to be guided by the nearness or distance at which the repetitions are placed in the original. When they follow too close one may vary the expression, but it is a question whether a professed translator be authorized to omit any. If they be tedious, the author is to answer for it.

It only remains to speak of the versification. Homer (as has been said) is perpetually applying the sound to the sense and varying it on every new subject. This is indeed one of the most exquisite beauties of poetry and attainable by very few; I know only of Homer eminent for it in the Greek, and Virgil in Latin. I am sensible it is what may sometimes happen by chance, when a writer is warm and fully possessed of his image; however, it may be reasonably believed they designed this in whose verse it so manifestly appears in a superior degree to all others. Few readers have the ear to be judges of it, but those who have will see I have endeavored at this beauty.

Upon the whole, I must confess myself utterly incapable of doing justice to Homer. I attempt him in no other hope but that which one may entertain without much vanity, of giving a more tolerable copy of him than any entire translation in verse has yet done. We have only those of Chapman, Hobbes, and Ogilby. Chapman has taken the advantage of an immeasurable length of verse, notwithstanding which there is scarce any paraphrase more loose and rambling than his. He has frequent interpolations of four or six lines, and I remember one in the thirteenth Book of the *Odysses*, v. 312, where he has spun twenty verses out of two. He is often mistaken in so bold a manner that one might think he deviated on purpose, if he did not in other places of his notes insist so much upon verbal trifles. He appears to have had a strong affectation of extracting new meanings out of his author, insomuch as to promise in his rhyming Preface a poem of the mysteries he had revealed in Homer; and perhaps he endeavored to strain the obvious sense to this end. His expression is involved in fustian, a fault for which he was remarkable in his original writings, as in the tragedy of *Bussy D'Ambois*, etc. In a word, the nature of the man may account for his whole performance; for he appears from his Preface and remarks to have been of an arrogant turn and an enthusiast in poetry. His own boast of having finished half the *Iliad* in less than fifteen weeks shows with what negligence his version was performed. But that which is to be allowed him and which very much contributed to cover his defects is a daring fiery spirit that animates his translation, which is something like what one might imagine Homer himself would have writ before he arrived to years of discretion. Hobbes has given us a correct explanation of the sense in general, but for particulars and circumstances he continually lops them and often omits the most beautiful. As for its being esteemed a close translation, I doubt not many have been led into that error by the shortness of it, which proceeds not from his following the original line by line but from the contractions above-mentioned. He sometimes omits whole similes and sentences, and is now and then guilty of mistakes which no writer of his learning could have fallen into but through carelessness. His poetry, as well as Ogilby's, is too mean for criticism.

It is a great loss to the poetical world that Mr. Dryden did not live to translate the *Iliad*. He has left us only the first book and a small part of the sixth, in which if he has in some places not truly interpreted the sense or preserved the antiquities, it ought to be excused on account of the haste he was obliged to write in. He seems to have had too much regard to Chapman, whose words he sometimes copies, and has unhappily followed him in passages where he wanders from the original. However, had he translated the whole work, I would no more have attempted Homer after him than Virgil, his version of whom (notwithstanding some human errors) is the most noble and spirited translation I know in any language. But the fate of great geniuses is like that of great ministers; though they are confessedly the first in the commonwealth of letters, they must be envied and calumniated only for being at the head of it.

That which in my opinion ought to be the endeavor of anyone who translates Homer is above all things to keep alive that spirit and fire which makes his chief character. In particular places, where the sense can bear any doubt, to follow the strongest and most poetical, as most agreeing with that character. To copy him in all the variations of his style and the different modulations of his numbers. To preserve in the more active or descriptive parts a warmth and elevation; in the more sedate or narrative, a plainness and solemnity; in the speeches a fullness and perspicuity; in the sentences a shortness and gravity. Not to neglect even the little figures and turns on the words, nor sometimes the very cast of the periods. Neither to omit or confound any rites or customs of antiquity. Perhaps too he ought to include the whole in a shorter compass than has hitherto been done by any translator who has tolerably preserved either the sense or poetry. What I would farther recommend to him is to study his author rather from his own text than from any commentaries, how learned soever, or whatever figure they make in the estimation of the world. To consider him attentively in comparison with Virgil above all the Ancients and with Milton above all the Moderns. Next these the Archbishop of Cambray's *Telemachus*[18] may give him the truest idea of the spirit and turn of our author, and Bossu's admirable treatise of the epic poem the justest notion of his design and conduct. But, after all, with whatever judgment and study a man may proceed or with whatever happiness he may perform such a work, he must hope to please but a few, those only who have at once a taste of poetry and competent learning. For to satisfy such as want either is not in the nature of this undertaking, since a mere modern wit can like nothing that is not modern, and a pedant nothing that is not Greek.

What I have done is submitted to the public, from whose opinions I am prepared to learn, though I fear no judges so little as our best poets, who are most sensible of the weight of this task. As for the worst, whatever they shall please to say, they may give me some concern as they are unhappy men, but none as they are malignant writers. I was guided in this translation by judgments very different from theirs and by persons for whom they can have no kindness, if an old observation be true, that the strongest antipathy in the world is that of fools to men of wit. Mr. Addison was the first whose advice determined me to undertake this task, who was pleased to write to me upon that occasion in such terms as I cannot repeat without vanity. I was obliged to Sir Richard Steele for a very early recommendation of my undertaking to the public. Dr. Swift promoted my interest with that warmth with which he always serves his friend. The humanity and frankness of Sir Samuel Garth are what I never knew wanting on any occasion. I must also acknowledge with infinite pleasure the many friendly offices as well as sincere criticisms of Mr. Congreve, who had led me the way in translating some parts of Homer, as I wish

18. François de Salignac de La Mothe Fénelon, *Télémaque* (1699).

for the sake of the world he had prevented[19] me in the rest. I must add the names of Mr. Rowe and Dr. Parnell, though I shall take a farther opportunity of doing justice to the last, whose good nature (to give it a great panegyric) is no less extensive than his learning. The favor of these gentlemen is not entirely undeserved by one who bears them so true an affection. But what can I say of the honor so many of the great have done me, while the first names of the age appear as my subscribers and the most distinguished patrons and ornaments of learning as my chief encouragers. Among these it is a particular pleasure to me to find that my highest obligations are to such who have done most honor to the name of poet, that his Grace the Duke of Buckingham was not displeased I should undertake the author to whom he has given (in his excellent *Essay*) the finest praise he ever yet received:

> Read Homer once, and you can read no more;
> For all things else appear so mean and poor,
> Verse will seem prose: yet often on him look,
> And you will hardly need another book.[20]

That the Earl of Halifax was one of the first to favor me, of whom it is hard to say whether the advancement of the polite arts is more owing to his generosity or his example. That such a genius as my Lord Bolingbroke, not more distinguished in the great scenes of business than in all the useful and entertaining parts of learning, has not refused to be the critic of these sheets and the patron of their writer. And that so excellent an imitator of Homer as the noble author of the tragedy of *Heroic Love*[21] has continued his partiality to me from my writing pastorals to my attempting the *Iliad*. I cannot deny myself the pride of confessing that I have had the advantage not only of their advice for the conduct in general, but their correction of several particulars of this translation.

I could say a great deal of the pleasure of being distinguished by the Earl of Carnarvon, but it is almost absurd to particularize

19. Anticipated.
20. John Sheffield, third Earl of Mulgrave, Duke of Buckingham, *An Essay upon Poetry* (1682), ll. 325–328.
21. George Granville, Lord Lansdowne.

any one generous action in a person whose whole life is a continued series of them. The Right Honorable Mr. Stanhope, the present Secretary of State, will pardon my desire of having it known that he was pleased to promote this affair. The particular zeal of Mr. Harcourt (the son of the late Lord Chancellor) gave me a proof how much I am honored in a share of his friendship. I must attribute to the same motive that of several others of my friends, to whom all acknowledgments are rendered unnecessary by the privileges of a familiar correspondence; and I am satisfied I can no way better oblige men of their turn than by my silence.

In short, I have found more patrons than ever Homer wanted. He would have thought himself happy to have met the same favor at Athens that has been shown me by its learned rival, the University of Oxford. If my author had the wits of after-ages for his defenders, his translator has had the beauties of the present for his advocates, a pleasure too great to be changed for any fame in reversion. And I can hardly envy him those pompous honors he received after death, when I reflect on the enjoyment of so many agreeable obligations and easy friendships which make the satisfaction of life. This distinction is the more to be acknowledged as it is shown to one whose pen has never gratified the prejudices of particular parties or the vanities of particular men. Whatever the success may prove, I shall never repent of an undertaking in which I have experienced the candor and friendship of so many persons of merit, and in which I hope to pass some of those years of youth that are generally lost in a circle of follies after a manner neither wholly unuseful to others nor disagreeable to myself.

From Pope's Observations on the *Iliad* (1715-1720)

ON CRITICS AND CRITICISM

It is something strange that of all the commentators upon Homer, there is hardly one whose principal design is to illustrate the poetical beauties of the author. They are voluminous in explaining those sciences which he made but subservient to his poetry, and sparing only upon that art which constitutes his character. This has been occasioned by the ostentation of men who had more reading than taste and were fonder of showing their variety of learning in all kinds than their single understanding in poetry. Hence it comes to pass that their remarks are rather philosophical, historical, geographical, allegorical, or in short rather anything than critical and poetical. . . . The chief design of the following notes is to comment upon Homer as a poet.

Opening note to Book I.

This comment by Macrobius is exactly in the spirit and almost in the cant of a true modern critic. The *simplicitas*, the *nescio quo modo*, the *genio antiqui poetae digna*[1] are excellent general phrases for those who have no reasons. "Simplicity" is our word of disguise for a shameful, unpoetical neglect of expression; the term of *je ne sais quoi* is the very support of all ignorant pretenders to delicacy; and to lift up our eyes and talk of the "genius of an Ancient" is at once the cheapest way of showing our own taste and the shortest way of criticizing the wit of others our contemporaries.

"Observations on the Catalogue," following Book II.

There is great strength, closeness, and spirit in this speech [of Ajax], and one might (like many critics) employ a whole page in

1. "Simplicity," "I know not how," "worthy of the genius of an ancient poet."

131

extolling and admiring it in general terms. But sure the perpetual rapture of such commentators, who are always giving us exclamations instead of criticisms, may be a mark of great admiration but of little judgment. Of what use is this either to a reader who has a taste or to one who has not? To admire a fine passage is what the former will do without us and what the latter cannot be taught to do by us. However, we ought gratefully to acknowledge the good nature of most people, who are not only pleased with this superficial applause given to fine passages, but are likewise inclined to transfer to the critic, who only points at these beauties, part of the admiration justly due to the poet. This is a cheap and easy way to fame, which many writers ancient and modern have pursued with great success. Formerly, indeed, this sort of authors had modesty and were humbly content to call their performances only *florilegia* or posies; but some of late have passed such collections on the world for criticisms of great depth and learning and seem to expect the same flowers should please us better in these paltry nosegays of their own making up than in the native gardens where they grew. As this practice of extolling without giving reasons is very convenient for most writers, so it excellently suits the ignorance or laziness of most readers, who will come into any sentiment rather than take the trouble of refuting it. Thus the compliment is mutual; for as such critics do not tax their readers with any thought to understand them, so their readers in return advance nothing in opposition to such critics. They may go roundly on, admiring and exclaiming in this manner: "What an exquisite spirit of poetry!" "How beautiful a circumstance!" "What delicacy of sentiments!" "With what art has the poet . . ." "In how sublime and just a manner . . ." "How finely imagined!" "How wonderfully beautiful and poetical!" And so proceed, without one reason to interrupt the course of their eloquence, most comfortably and ignorantly apostrophising to the end of the chapter.

Book XV, 1. 890.

ON DESIGN

It may be proper here to take a general view of the conduct of the *Iliad*. The whole design turns upon the wrath of Achilles; that wrath is not to be appeased but by the calamities of the Greeks, who are taught by their frequent defeats the importance of this hero; for in epic, as in tragic poetry, there ought to be some evident and necessary incident at the winding up of the catastrophe, and that should be founded upon some visible distress. This conduct has an admirable effect, not only as it gives an air of probability to the relation, by allowing leisure to the wrath of Achilles to cool and die away by degrees (who is everywhere described as a person of a stubborn resentment and consequently ought not to be easily reconciled), but also as it highly contributes to the honor of Achilles, which was to be fully satisfied before he could relent.

Opening note to Book XII.

The quarrel having risen to its highest extravagance, Nestor, the wisest and most aged Greek, is raised to quiet the Princes, whose speech is therefore framed entirely with an opposite air to all which has been hitherto said, sedate and inoffensive. . . . It was not however consistent with the plan of the poem that this should entirely appease them, for then the anger would be at an end which was proposed to be sung through the whole. Homer has not therefore made this speech to have its full success; and yet that the eloquence of his Nestor might not be thrown out of character by its proving unavailable, he takes care that the violence with which the dispute was managed should abate immediately upon his speaking; Agamemnon confesses that all he spoke was right, Achilles promises not to fight for Briseis if she should be sent for, and the council dissolves.

Book I, l. 339.

As in every just history-picture there is one principal figure to which all the rest refer and are subservient, so in each battle of the *Iliad* there is one principal person that may properly be called the hero of that day or action. This conduct preserves the unity of the piece and keeps the imagination from being distracted and confused with a wild number of independent figures, which have no subordination to each other. To make this probable, Homer supposes these extraordinary measures of courage to be the immediate gift of the gods, who bestow them sometimes upon one, and sometimes upon another, as they think fit to make them the instruments of their designs, an opinion conformable to true theology. Whoever reflects upon this will not blame our author for representing the same heroes brave at one time and dispirited at another, just as the gods assist or abandon them on different occasions.

Opening note to Book V.

It must be owned that a surprise artfully managed, which arises from unexpected revolutions of great actions, affects the mind with a peculiar delight.[2] In this consists the principal pleasure of a romance and well-writ tragedy. But besides this, there is in the relation of great events a different kind of pleasure, which arises from the artful unravelling a knot of actions which we knew before in the gross. This is a delight peculiar to history and epic poetry, which is founded on history. In these kinds of writing, a preceding summary knowledge of the events described does no way damp our curiosity, but rather makes it more eager for the detail. This is evident in a good history, where generally the reader is affected with a greater delight in proportion to his preceding knowledge of the facts described: the pleasure in this case is like that of an architect first viewing some magnificent building, who was before well acquainted with the proportions of it. In an epic poem the case is of a like nature, where, as if the historical foreknowledge were not sufficient, the most judicious poets never fail to excite their reader's curiosity by some small sketches of their design, which, like the outlines of a fine picture, will necessarily raise in us a greater desire to see it in its finished coloring.

Book XV, l. 67.

2. Pope is here answering the criticism that Homer, by permitting Jupiter to describe events to come, inartistically takes away the element of surprise.

This [Book XXIII] and the following book, which contain the description of the funeral of Patroclus and other matters relating to Hector, are undoubtedly superadded to the grand catastrophe of the poem; for the story is completely finished with the death of that hero in the twenty-second book. Many judicious critics have been of opinion that Homer is blamable for protracting it. Virgil closes the whole scene of action with the death of Turnus and leaves the rest to be imagined by the mind of the reader; he does not draw the picture at full length but delineates it so far that we cannot fail of imagining the whole draught. There is, however, one thing to be said in favor of Homer which may perhaps justify him in his method, that what he undertook to paint was the *anger* of Achilles; and as that anger does not die with Hector but persecutes his very remains, so the poet still keeps up to his subject; nay, it seems to require that he should carry down the relation of that resentment which is the foundation of his poem till it is fully satisfied; and as this survives Hector and gives the poet an opportunity of still showing many sad effects of Achilles's anger, the two following books may be thought not to be excrescencies but essential to the poem.

Opening note to Book XXIII.

ON THE MORAL

I think it necessary to take notice to the reader that nothing is more admirable than the conduct of Homer throughout his whole poem in respect to morality. He justifies the character of Horace, "who tells us what is fair, what is foul, what is helpful, what not, more plainly and better than Chrysippus or Crantor."[3] If the reader does not observe the morality of the *Ilias*, he loses half and the nobler part of its beauty: he reads it as a common romance and mistakes the chief aim of it, which is to instruct.

Book XXIV, l. 519.

I confess it is a satisfaction to me to observe with what art the poet pursues his subject. The opening of the poem professes to

3. *Quid pulchrum, quid turpe, quid utile, quid non,*
   plenius et melius Chrysippo et Crantore dicit.
Epistles, I, ii, 3–4. Translation by Fairclough.

treat of the anger of Achilles; that anger draws on all the great events of the story, and Homer at every opportunity awakens the reader to an attention to it by mentioning the effects of it; so that when we see in this place the hero deaf to youth and compassion it is what we expect. Mercy in him would offend, because it is contrary to his character. Homer proposes him not as a pattern for imitation; but the moral of the poem which he designed the reader should draw from it is that we should avoid anger, since it is ever pernicious in the event.

Book XX, 1. 541.

This is one, among a thousand instances, of Homer's indirect and oblique manner of introducing moral sentences and instructions. These agreeably break in upon his reader even in descriptions and poetical parts, where one naturally expects only painting and amusement. We have virtue put upon us by surprise and are pleased to find a thing where we should never have looked to meet with it. I must do a noble English poet[4] the justice to observe that it is this particular art that is the very distinguishing excellence of *Cooper's Hill*, throughout which the descriptions of places and images raised by the poet are still tending to some hint or leading into some reflection upon moral life or political institution, much in the same manner as the real sight of such scenes and prospects is apt to give the mind a composed turn and incline it to thoughts and contemplations that have a relation to the object.

Book XVI, 1. 466.

ON CHARACTERIZATION

We should know that the poet has rather studied Nature than perfection in the laying down his characters. He resolved to sing the consequences of anger; he considered what virtues and vices would conduce most to bring his moral out of the fable and artfully disposed them in his chief persons after the manner in which we generally find them, making the fault which most peculiarly attends any good quality to reside with it. Thus he has

4. Sir John Denham.

placed pride with magnanimity in Agamemnon, and craft with prudence in Ulysses. And thus we must take his Achilles, not as a mere heroic dispassioned character but as compounded of courage and anger, one who finds himself almost invincible and assumes an uncontrolled carriage upon the self-consciousness of his worth, whose high strain of honor will not suffer him to betray his friends or fight against them, even when he thinks they have affronted him, but whose inexorable resentment will not let him hearken to any terms of accommodation. These are the lights and shades of his character, which Homer has heightened and darkened in extremes, because on the one side valor is the darling quality of epic poetry and, on the other, anger the particular subject of his poem. When characters thus mixed are well conducted, though they be not morally beautiful quite through, they conduce more to the end and are still poetically perfect.

Book I, l. 155.

There are several reasons which render Hector a favorite character with every reader, some of which shall here be offered. The chief moral of Homer was to expose the ill effects of discord; the Greeks were to be shown disunited, and to render that disunion the more probable, he has designedly given them *mixed* characters. The Trojans, on the other hand, were to be represented making all advantages of the others disagreement, which they could not do without a strict union among themselves. Hector, therefore, who commanded them, must be endued with all such qualifications as tended to the preservation of it, as Achilles with such as promoted the contrary. The one stands, in contrast to the other, an accomplished character of valor unruffled by rage and anger, and uniting his people by his prudence and example. Hector has also a foil to set him off in his own family; we are perpetually opposing in our minds the incontinence of Paris, who exposes his country, to the temperance of Hector, who protects it. And indeed it is this love of his country which appears his principal passion and the motive of all his actions. He has no other blemish than that he fights in an unjust cause, which Homer has yet been careful to tell us he would not do if his opinion were followed. But since he cannot prevail, the affection he bears to his parents and kindred and his desire of defending them incites him to do his utmost for their safety. We may add that Homer having so many Greeks to celebrate makes them shine in their turns and singly in their several books, one succeeding in the absence of another; whereas Hector appears in every battle the life and soul of his party and the constant bulwark against every enemy: he stands against Agamemnon's magnanimity, Diomed's bravery, Ajax's strength, and Achilles's fury.

                                                        Book III, 1. 53.

As Homer's invention is in nothing more wonderful than in the great variety of characters with which his poems are diversified, so his judgment appears in nothing more exact than in that propriety with which each character is maintained. But this exactness must be collected by a diligent attention to his conduct through the whole; and when the particulars of each character are laid together, we shall find them all proceeding from the same temper and disposition of the person. If this observation be neglected, the poet's conduct will lose much of its true beauty and harmony.

                                                  Book XI, opening note.

ON IMAGERY

Those critics who fancy that the use of comparisons distracts the attention and draws it from the first image which should most employ it (as that we lose the idea of the battle itself while we are led by a simile to that of a deluge or a storm), those, I say, may as well imagine we lose the thought of the sun when we see his reflection in the water, where he appears more distinctly and is contemplated more at ease than if we gazed directly at his beams. For 'tis with the eye of the imagination as with our corporeal eye, it must sometimes be taken off from the object in order to see it the better. The same critics that are displeased to have their fancy distracted (as they call it) are yet so inconsistent with themselves as to object to Homer that his similes are too much alike and are too often derived from the same animal. But is it not more reasonable (according to their own notion) to compare the same man always to the same animal than to see him sometimes a sun, sometimes a tree, and sometimes a river? Though Homer speaks of the same creature, he so diversifies the circumstances and accidents of the comparisons that they always appear quite different. And to say truth, it is not so much the animal or the thing as the action or posture of them that employs our imagination: two different animals in the same action are more like to each other than one and the same animal is to himself in two different actions. And those who in reading Homer are shocked that 'tis always a *lion* may as well be angry that 'tis always a *man*.

What may seem more exceptionable is his inserting the same comparisons in the same words at length upon different occasions, by which management he makes one single image afford many ornaments to several parts of the poem. But may not one say Homer is in this like a skilful improver, who places a beautiful statue in a well-disposed garden so as to answer several vistas, and by that artifice one single figure seems multiplied into as many objects as there are openings from whence it may be viewed?

From "An Essay on Homer's Battles," following Book IV.

> Thus by their leader's care each martial band
> Moves into ranks and stretches o'er the land.
> With shouts the Trojans rushing from afar,
> Proclaim their motions, and provoke the war:
> So when inclement winters vex the plain
> With piercing frosts, or thick-descending rain,
> To warmer seas the cranes embodied fly,
> With noise, and order, thro' the mid-way sky;
> To pigmy nations wounds and death they bring,
> And all the war descends upon the wing.
> (Book III, ll. 1–10)

If wit has been truly described to be a similitude in ideas and is more excellent as that similitude is more surprising, there cannot be a truer kind of wit than what is shown in apt comparisons, especially when composed of such subjects as having the least relation to each other in general have yet some particular that agrees exactly. Of this nature is the simile of the cranes to the Trojan army, where the fancy of Homer flew to the remotest part of the world for an image which no reader could have expected. But it is no less exact than surprising. The likeness consists in two points, the *noise* and the *order*; the latter is so observable as to have given some of the ancients occasion to imagine the embattling of an army was first learned from the close manner of flight of these birds. But this part of the simile not being directly expressed by the author has been overlooked by some of the commentators. It may be remarked that Homer has generally a wonderful closeness in all the particulars of his comparisons, notwithstanding he takes a liberty in his expression of them. He seems so secure of the main likeness that he makes no scruple to play with the circumstances, sometimes by transposing the order of them, sometimes by superadding them, and sometimes (as in this place) by neglecting them in such a manner as to leave the reader to supply them himself.

Book III, 1. 7.

One may make a general observation that Homer in those comparisons that breathe an air of tenderness is very exact and adapts them in every point to the subject which he is to illustrate; but in other comparisons, where he is to inspire the soul with sublime sentiments, he gives a loose to his fancy and does not regard whether the images exactly correspond. I take the reason of it to be this: in the first, the copy must be like the original to cause it to affect us; the glass needs only to return the real image to make it beautiful; whereas in the other, a succession of noble ideas will cause the like sentiments in the soul, and though the glass should enlarge the image, it only strikes us with such thoughts as the poet intended to raise, sublime and great.

Book VIII, 1. 370.

> As from some mountain's craggy forehead torn,
> A rock's round fragment flies, with fury borne,
> (Which from the stubborn stone a torrent rends),
> Precipitate the pond'rous mass descends:
> From steep to steep the rolling ruin bounds;
> At ev'ry shock the crackling wood resounds;
> Still gath'ring force, it smokes; and, urged amain,

Whirls, leaps, and thunders down, impetuous to the plain:
There stops—So Hector.
(Book XIII, ll. 191–199)

This is one of the noblest similes in all Homer, and the most justly corresponding in its circumstances to the thing described. The furious descent of Hector from the wall represented by a stone that flies from the top of a rock, the hero pushed on by the superior force of Jupiter, as the stone driven by a torrent; the ruins of the wall falling after him, all things yielding before him, the clamor and tumult around him, all imaged in the violent bounding and leaping of the stone, the crackling of the woods, the shock, the noise, the rapidity, the irresistibility, and the augmentation of force in its progress: all these points of likeness make but the first part of this admirable simile. Then the sudden stop of the stone when it comes to the plain, as of Hector at the phalanx of the Ajaces (alluding also to the natural situation of the ground, Hector rushing down the declivity of the shore and being stopped on the level of the sea) and, lastly, the immobility of both when so stopped, the enemy being as unable to move him back as he to get forward: this last branch of the comparison is the happiest in the world, and, though not hitherto observed, is what methinks makes the principal beauty and force of it.

Book XIII, l. 191.

As when old Ocean's silent surface sleeps,
The waves just heaving on the purple deeps;
While yet th' expected tempest hangs on high,
Weighs down the cloud, and blackens in the sky,
The mass of waters will no wind obey;
Jove sends one gust, and bids them roll away.
While wav'ring counsels thus his mind engage,
Fluctuates, in doubtful thought, the Pylian sage.
(Book XIV, ll. 21–28)

There are nowhere more finished pictures of nature than those which Homer draws in several of his comparisons. The beauty, however, of some of these will be lost to many, who cannot perceive the resemblance, having never had opportunity to observe the things themselves. The life of this description will be most sensible to those who have been at sea in a calm; in this condition the water is not entirely motionless, but swells gently in smooth waves, which fluctuate backwards and forwards in a kind of balancing motion: this state continues till a rising wind gives a determination to the waves and rolls them one certain way. There is scarce anything in the whole compass of nature that can more exactly represent the state of an irresolute mind, wavering between two different designs, sometimes inclining to the one, sometimes to the other, and then moving to that point to which its resolution is at last determined. Every circumstance of this comparison is both beautiful and just; and it is the more to be admired because it is very difficult to find sensible images proper to represent the motions of the mind, wherefore we but rarely meet with such comparisons even in the best poets.

Book XIV, 1. 21.

> Not half so loud the bellowing deeps resound,
> When stormy winds disclose the dark profound;
> Less loud the winds, that from th'Aeolian hall
> Roar thro' the woods, and make whole forests fall;
> Less loud the woods, when flames in torrents pour,
> Catch the dry mountain, and its shades devour:
> With such a rage the meeting hosts are driven,
> And such a clamor shakes the sounding heaven.
>
> (Book XIV, ll. 457–464)

This passage cannot be thought justly liable to the objections which have been made against heaping comparisons one upon another, whereby the principal object is lost amidst too great a variety of different images. In this case the principal image is more strongly impressed on the mind by a multiplication of similes, which are the natural product of an imagination laboring to express something very vast, but, finding no single idea sufficient to answer its conceptions, it endeavors by redoubling the comparisons to supply this defect: the different sounds of waters, winds, and flames being as it were united in one. We have several instances of this sort even in so castigated and reserved a writer as Virgil.

Book XIV, 1. 457.

This simile translated literally runs thus: "As the numerous troops of flies about a shepherd's cottage in the spring, when the milk moistens the pails; such numbers of Greeks stood in the field against the Trojans, desiring their destruction." The lowness of this image, in comparison with those which precede it, will naturally shock a modern critic and would scarce be forgiven in a poet of these times. The utmost a translator can do is to heighten the expression so as to render the disparity less observable, which is endeavored here and in other places. If this be done successfully, the reader is so far from being offended at a low idea, that it raises his surprise to find it grown great in the poet's hands, of which we have frequent instances in Virgil's *Georgics*.

Book II, l. 552.

To judge rightly of comparisons, we are not to examine if the subject from whence they are derived be great or little, noble or familiar; but we are principally to consider if the image produced be clear and lively, if the poet has the skill to dignify it by poetical words, and if it perfectly paints the thing it is intended to represent.

Book XI, l. 669.

ON PAINTING AND POETRY

There never was a finer piece of painting than this. Hector extends his arms to embrace his child; the child, affrighted at the glittering of his helmet and the shaking of the plume, shrinks backward to the breast of his nurse; Hector unbraces his helmet, lays it on the ground, takes the infant in his arms, lifts him towards heaven, and offers a prayer for him to the gods; then returns him to the mother Andromache, who receives him with a smile of pleasure, but at the same instant the fears for her husband make her burst into tears. All these are but small circumstances, but so artfully chosen that every reader immediately feels the force of them and represents the whole in the utmost liveliness to his imagination. This alone might be a confutation of that false criticism some have fallen into, who affirm that a poet ought only to collect the great and noble particulars in his paintings. But it is in the images of things as in the characters of persons; where a small action or even a small circumstance of an action lets us more into the knowledge and comprehension of them than the material and principal parts themselves. As we find this in a history, so we do in a picture, where sometimes a small motion or turning of a finger will express the character and action of the figure more than all the other parts of the design. Longinus indeed blames an author's insisting too much on trivial circumstances, but in the same place extols Homer as "the poet who best knew how to make use of important and beautiful circumstances and to avoid the mean and superfluous ones." There is a vast difference betwixt a *small* circumstance and a *trivial* one, and the smallest become important if they are well chosen and not confused.

Book VI, 1. 595.

Homer has a wonderful art and judgment in contriving such incidents as set the characteristic qualities of his heroes in the highest point of light. There is hardly any in the whole *Iliad* more proper to move pity than this circumstance of Lycaon, or to raise terror than this view of Achilles. It is also the finest picture of them both imaginable. We see the different attitude of their persons, and the different passions which appeared in their countenances: at first Achilles stands erect, with surprise in his looks at the sight of one whom he thought it impossible to find there, while Lycaon is in the posture of a suppliant, with looks that plead for compassion, with one hand holding the hero's lance and his knee with the other; afterwards, when at his death he lets go the spear and places himself on his knees with his arms extended to receive the mortal wound, how lively and how strongly is this painted? I believe everyone perceives the beauty of this passage and allows that poetry (at least in Homer) is truly a speaking picture.[5]

Book XXI, 1. 41.

5. A famous phrase attributed to Simonides of Ceos (*ca.* 556–467 B.C.).

ON SOUND AND SENSE

There is a great beauty in the versification of this whole passage in Homer; some of the verses run hoarse, full, and sonorous, like the torrent they describe; others, by their broken cadences and sudden stops, image the difficulty, labor, and interruption of the hero's march against it. The fall of the elm, the tearing up of the bank, the rushing of the branches in the water, are all put into such words that almost every letter corresponds in its sound and echoes to the sense of each particular.

Book XXI, l. 264.

> Bending he fell, and doubled to the ground,
> Lay panting.

The original is,

> ὁ δ' ἐσπόμενος περὶ δουρὶ
> ἤσπαιρ'

The versification represents the short broken pantings of the dying warrior in the short sudden break at the second syllable of the second line. And this beauty is, as it happens, precisely copied in the English. It is not often that a translator can do this justice to Homer, but he must be content to imitate these graces and proprieties at more distance by endeavoring at something parallel, though not the same.

Book XIII, l. 721.

ON HOMER'S BOLD INVENTION

> Mars bellows with the pain:
> Loud as the roar encount'ring armies yield,
> When shouting millions shake the thund'ring field.
> Both armies start, and trembling gaze around;
> And earth and heaven rebellow to the sound.
> (Book V, ll. 1053–1057)

This hyperbole to express the roaring of Mars, so strong as it is, yet is not extravagant. It wants not a qualifying circumstance or two; the voice is not human, but that of a deity, and the comparison being taken from an army renders it more natural with respect to the God of War. It is less daring to say that a god could send forth a voice as loud as the shout of two armies than that Camilla, a Latian nymph, could run so swiftly over the corn as not to bend an ear of it; or, to allege a nearer instance, that Polyphemus, a mere mortal, shook all the island of Sicily and made the deepest caverns of Aetna roar with his cries.[6] Yet Virgil generally escapes the censure of those moderns who are shocked with the bold flights of Homer. It is usual with those who are slaves to common opinion to overlook or praise the same things in one that they blame in another. They think to depreciate Homer in extolling the judgment of Virgil, who never showed it more than when he followed him in these boldnesses. And indeed they who would take boldness from poetry must leave dullness in the room of it.

Book V, l. 1054.

Upon the whole we may observe that it seems not only the fate of great geniuses to have met with the most malignant critics, but of the finest and noblest passages in them to have been particularly pitched upon for impertinent criticisms. These are the divine boldnesses which in their very nature provoke ignorance and short-sightedness to show themselves, and which whoever is capable of attaining must also certainly know that they will be attacked by such as cannot reach them.

Book IV, l. 503.

6. Pope alludes to *Aeneid*, VII, 808 ff., and III, 672–674.

Postscript to the *Odyssey* (1726)

I cannot dismiss this work without a few observations on the true character and style of it. Whoever reads the *Odyssey* with an eye to the *Iliad*, expecting to find it of the same character or of the same sort of spirit, will be grievously deceived and err against the first principle of criticism, which is to consider the nature of the piece and the intent of its author. The *Odyssey* is a moral and political work, instructive to all degrees of men and filled with images, examples, and precepts of civil and domestic life. Homer is here a person "who has learned what he owes his country and his friends, what love is due a parent, a brother, and a guest; who tells us what is fair, what is foul, what is helpful, what not, more plainly and better than Chrysippus or Crantor."[1] The *Odyssey* is the reverse of the *Iliad* in moral, subject, manner, and style, to which it has no sort of relation but as the story happens to follow in order of time and as some of the same persons are actors in it. Yet from this incidental connection many have been misled to regard it as a continuation or second part, and thence to expect a parity of character inconsistent with its nature.

It is no wonder that the common reader should fall into this mistake, when so great a critic as Longinus seems not wholly free from it, although what he has said has been generally understood to import a severer censure of the *Odyssey* than it really does, if we consider the occasion on which it is introduced and the circumstances to which it is confined.

1. *Qui didicit, patriae quid debeat et quid amicis,*
   quo sit amore parens, quo frater amandus, et hospes

   Horace *Ars Poetica*, 312–313.
   Qui quid sit pulchrum, quid turpe, quid utile, quid non,
   plenius et melius Chrysippo et Crantore dicit.

   Horace *Epist.* I. ii, 3–4.
   Translation by Fairclough.

147

"The *Odyssey*," says he, "is an instance, how natural it is to a great genius, when it begins to grow old and decline, to delight itself in narrations and fables. For, that Homer composed the *Odyssey* after the *Iliad* many proofs may be given, etc. From hence in my judgment it proceeds that as the *Iliad* was written while his spirit was in its greatest vigor, the whole structure of that work is dramatic and full of action, whereas the greater part of the *Odyssey* is employed in narration, which is the taste of old age; so that in this latter piece we may compare him to the setting sun, which has still the same greatness but not the same ardor or force. He speaks not in the same strain; we see no more that sublime of the *Iliad* which marches on with a constant pace without ever being stopped or retarded; there appears no more that hurry and that strong tide of motions and passions, pouring one after another; there is no more the same fury or the same volubility of diction, so suitable to action, and all along drawing in such innumerable images of nature. But Homer, like the ocean, is always great, even when he ebbs and retires, even when he is lowest, and loses himself most in narrations and incredible fictions; as instances of this, we cannot forget the descriptions of tempests, the adventures of Ulysses with the Cyclops, and many others. But though all this be age, it is the age of Homer. And it may be said for the credit of these fictions that they are beautiful dreams, or if you will, the dreams of Jupiter himself. I spoke of the *Odyssey* only to show that the greatest poets, when their genius wants strength and warmth for the pathetic, for the most part employ themselves in painting the manners. This Homer has done, in characterizing the suitors and describing their way of life, which is properly a branch of comedy, whose peculiar business it is to represent the manners of men."[2]

We must first observe it is the sublime of which Longinus is writing; that, and not the nature of Homer's poem, is his subject. After having highly extolled the sublimity and fire of the *Iliad*, he justly observes the *Odyssey* to have less of those qualities and to turn more on the side of moral, and reflections on human life. Nor is it his business here to determine whether the elevated

2. *On the Sublime*, Sect. IX.

spirit of the one or the just moral of the other be the greater excellence in itself.

Secondly, that fire and fury of which he is speaking cannot well be meant of the general spirit and inspiration which is to run through a whole epic poem, but of that particular warmth and impetuosity necessary in some parts to image or represent actions or passions of haste, tumult, and violence. It is on occasion of citing some such particular passages in Homer that Longinus breaks into this reflection, which seems to determine his meaning chiefly to that sense.

Upon the whole, he affirms the *Odyssey* to have less sublimity and fire than the *Iliad*, but he does not say it wants the sublime or wants fire. He affirms it to be narrative, but not that the narration is defective. He affirms it to abound in fictions, not that those fictions are ill invented or ill executed. He affirms it to be nice and particular in painting the manners, but not that those manners are ill painted. If Homer has fully in these points accomplished his own design and done all that the nature of his poem demanded or allowed, it still remains perfect in its kind and as much a masterpiece as the *Iliad*. The amount of the passage is this: that in his own particular taste, and with respect to the sublime, Longinus preferred the *Iliad*; and because the *Odyssey* was less active and lofty, he judged it the work of the old age of Homer.

If this opinion be true, it will only prove that Homer's age might determine him in the choice of his subject, but not that it affected him in the execution of it; and that which would be a very wrong instance to prove the decay of his imagination is a very good one to evince the strength of his judgment. For had he (as Madame Dacier observes) composed the *Odyssey* in his youth and the *Iliad* in his age, both must in reason have been exactly the same as they now stand. To blame Homer for his choice of such a subject as did not admit the same incidents and the same pomp of style as his former is to take offence at too much variety and to imagine that when a man has written one good thing, he must ever after only copy himself.

The "Battle of Constantine" and the "School of Athens" are

both pieces of Raphael; shall we censure the "School of Athens" as faulty because it has not the fury and fire of the other? Or shall we say that Raphael was grown grave and old because he chose to represent the manners of old men and philosophers? There is all the silence, tranquillity, and composure in the one, and all the warmth, hurry, and tumult in the other, which the subject of either required: both of them had been imperfect if they had not been as they are. And let the painter or poet be young or old who designs and performs in this manner, it proves him to have made the piece at a time of life when he was master not only of his art but of his discretion.

Aristotle makes no such distinction between the two poems: he constantly cites them with equal praise and draws the rules and examples of epic writing equally from both. But it is rather to the *Odyssey* that Horace gives the preference in the *Epistle to Lollius* and in the *Art of Poetry*.[3] It is remarkable how opposite his opinion is to that of Longinus, and that the particulars he chooses to extol are those very fictions and pictures of the manners which the other seems least to approve. Those fables and manners are of the very essence of the work, but even without that regard, the fables themselves have both more invention and more instruction, and the manners more moral and example, than those of the *Iliad*.

In some points (and those the most essential to the epic poem) the *Odyssey* is confessed to excel the *Iliad*, and principally in the great end of it, the moral. The conduct, turn, and disposition of the *fable* is also what the critics allow to be the better model for epic writers to follow; accordingly, we find much more of the cast of this poem than of the other in the *Aeneid* and (what next to that is perhaps the greatest example) in the *Telemachus*.[4] In the *manners* it is no way inferior; Longinus is so far from finding any defect in these that he rather taxes Homer with painting them too minutely. As to the *narrations*, although they are more numerous as the occasions are more frequent, yet they carry no more the marks of old age, and are neither more prolix nor more

3. *Epist.* I. ii. The reference to the *Ars Poetica* is not clear.
4. *Télémaque* by Fénelon (1699).

circumstantial, than the conversations and dialogues of the *Iliad*. Not to mention the length of those of Phoenix in the Ninth Book, and of Nestor in the Eleventh (which may be thought in compliance to their characters), those of Glaucus in the Sixth, of Aeneas in the Twentieth, and some others, must be allowed to exceed any in the whole *Odyssey*. And that the propriety of style and the numbers in the narrations of each are equal will appear to any who compare them.

To form a right judgment whether the genius of Homer had suffered any decay, we must consider, in both his poems, such parts as are of a similar nature and will bear comparison. And it is certain we shall find in each the same vivacity and fecundity of invention, the same life and strength of imaging and coloring, the particular descriptions as highly painted, the figures as bold, the metaphors as animated, and the numbers as harmonious and as various.

The *Odyssey* is a perpetual source of poetry; the stream is not the less full for being gentle, though it is true (when we speak only with regard to the sublime) that a river foaming and thundering in cataracts from rocks and precipices is what more strikes, amazes, and fills the mind than the same body of water flowing afterwards through peaceful vales and agreeable scenes of pasturage.

The *Odyssey* (as I have before said) ought to be considered according to its own nature and design, not with an eye to the *Iliad*. To censure Homer because it is unlike what it was never meant to resemble is as if a gardener who had purposely cultivated two beautiful trees of contrary natures, as a specimen of his skill in the several kinds, should be blamed for not bringing them into pairs; when in root, stem, leaf, and flower each was so entirely different that one must have been spoiled in the endeavor to match the other.

Longinus, who saw this poem was "partly of the nature of comedy," ought not for that very reason to have considered it with a view to the *Iliad*.[5] How little any such resemblance was the intention of Homer may appear from hence, that although the

5. *On the Sublime*, Sect. IX.

character of Ulysses there was already drawn, yet here he purposely turns to another side of it and shows him, not in that full
light of glory, but in the shade of common life, with a mixture
of such qualities as are requisite to all the lowest accidents of it,
struggling with misfortunes, and on a level with the meanest of
mankind. As for the other persons, none of them are above what
we call the higher comedy: Calypso, though a goddess, is a character of intrigue; the suitors are yet more approaching to it; the
Phaecians are of the same cast; the Cyclops, Melanthius, and Irus
descend even to droll characters; and the scenes that appear
throughout are generally of the comic kind: banquets, revels,
sports, loves, and the pursuit of a woman.

From the nature of the poem, we shall form an idea of the
style. The diction is to follow the images and to take its color
from the complexion of the thoughts. Accordingly, the *Odyssey* is
not always clothed in the majesty of verse proper to tragedy, but
sometimes descends into the plainer narrative, and sometimes
even to that familiar dialogue essential to comedy. However,
where it cannot support a sublimity, it always preserves a dignity
or at least a propriety.

There is a real beauty in an easy, pure, perspicuous description even of a low action. There are numerous instances of this
both in Homer and Virgil, and perhaps those natural passages
are not the least pleasing of their works. It is often the same in
history, where the representations of common or even domestic
things in clear, plain, and natural words, are frequently found
to make the liveliest impression on the reader.

The question is how far a poet, in pursuing the description
or image of an action, can attach himself to little circumstances
without vulgarity or trifling. What particulars are proper and
enliven the image? Or what are impertinent and clog it? In this
matter painting is to be consulted, and the whole regard had to
those circumstances which contribute to form a full, and yet not
a confused, idea of the thing.

Epithets are of vast service to this effect, and the right use of
these is often the only expedient to render the narration poetical.

The great point of judgment is to distinguish when to speak

simply and when figuratively; but whenever the poet is obliged by the nature of his subject to descend to the lower manner of writing, an elevated style would be affected and therefore ridiculous; and the more he was forced upon figures and metaphors to avoid that lowness, the more the image would be broken and consequently obscure.

One may add that the use of the grand style on little subjects is not only ludicrous but a sort of transgression against the rules of proportion and mechanics: 'tis using a vast force to lift a feather.

I believe, now I am upon this head, it will be found a just observation that the low actions of life cannot be put into a figurative style without being ridiculous, but things natural can. Metaphors raise the latter into dignity, as we see in the *Georgics*, but throw the former into ridicule, as in the *Lutrin*.[6] I think this may very well be accounted for: laughter implies censure; inanimate and irrational beings are not objects of censure. Therefore these may be elevated as much as you please, and no ridicule follows; but when rational beings are represented above their real character, it becomes ridiculous in art because it is vicious in morality. The bees in Virgil, were they rational beings, would be ridiculous by having their actions and manners represented on a level with creatures so superior as men, since it would imply folly or pride, which are the proper objects of ridicule.

The use of pompous expression for low actions or thoughts is the true sublime of *Don Quixote*. How far unfit it is for epic poetry appears in its being the perfection of the mock-epic. It is so far from being the sublime of tragedy that it is the cause of all bombast, when poets, instead of being (as they imagine) constantly lofty, only preserve throughout a painful equality of fustian; that continued swell of language which runs indiscriminately even through their lowest characters and rattles like some mightiness of meaning in the most indifferent subjects is of a piece with that perpetual elevation of tone which the players have learned from it, and which is not speaking, but vociferating.[7]

6. Mock-heroic poem by Boileau (1674).
7. Cf. Pope's letter to the Earl of Oxford, p. 39.

There is still more reason for a variation of style in epic poetry than in tragic, to distinguish between that language of the gods proper to the muse who sings and is inspired, and that of men who are introduced speaking only according to nature. Farther, there ought to be a difference of style observed in the speeches of human persons and those of deities; and again, in those which may be called set harangues or orations, and those which are only conversation or dialogue. Homer has more of the latter than any other poet; what Virgil does by two or three words of narration, Homer still performs by speeches; not only replies but even rejoinders are frequent in him, a practice almost unknown to Virgil. This renders his poems more animated but less grave and majestic, and consequently necessitates the frequent use of a lower style. The writers of tragedy lie under the same necessity if they would copy nature, whereas that painted and poetical diction which they perpetually use would be improper even in orations designed to move with all the arts of rhetoric. This is plain from the practice of Demosthenes and Cicero; and Virgil in those of Drances and Turnus gives an eminent example how far removed the style of them ought to be from such an excess of figures and ornaments, which indeed fits only that language of the gods we have been speaking of, or that of a muse under inspiration.

To read through a whole work in this strain is like traveling all along on the ridge of a hill, which is not half so agreeable as sometimes gradually to rise, and sometimes gently to descend, as the way leads and as the end of the journey directs.

Indeed the true reason that so few poets have imitated Homer in these lower parts has been the extreme difficulty of preserving that mixture of ease and dignity essential to them. For it is as hard for an epic poem to stoop to the narrative with success as for a prince to descend to be familiar without diminution to his greatness.

The sublime style is more easily counterfeited than the natural; something that passes for it, or sounds like it, is common in all false writers. But nature, purity, perspicuity, and simplicity never walk in the clouds; they are obvious to all capacities; and where they are not evident, they do not exist.

The most plain narration not only admits of these and of harmony (which are all the qualities of style), but it requires every one of them to render it pleasing. On the contrary, whatever pretends to a share of the sublime may pass, notwithstanding any defects in the rest, nay, sometimes without any of them, and gain the admiration of all ordinary readers.

Homer, in his lowest narrations or speeches, is ever easy, flowing, copious, clear, and harmonious. He shows not less invention in assembling the humbler than the greater thoughts and images; nor less judgment in proportioning the style and the versification to these than to the other. Let it be remembered that the same genius that soared the highest, and from whom the greatest models of the sublime are derived, was also he who stooped the lowest and gave to the simple narrative its utmost perfection. Which of these was the harder task to Homer himself I cannot pretend to determine; but to his translator I can affirm (however unequal all his imitations must be) that of the latter has been much the more difficult.

Whoever expects here the same pomp of verse and the same ornaments of diction as in the *Iliad*, he will, and he ought to be, disappointed. Were the original otherwise, it had been an offence against nature; and were the translation so, it were an offence against Homer, which is the same thing.

It must be allowed that there is a majesty and harmony in the Greek language which greatly contribute to elevate and support the narration. But I must also observe that this is an advantage grown upon the language since Homer's time, for things are removed from vulgarity by being out of use; and if the words we could find in any present language were equally sonorous or musical in themselves, they would still appear less poetical and uncommon than those of a dead one, from this only circumstance of being in every man's mouth. I may add to this another disadvantage to a translator, from a different cause: Homer seems to have taken upon him the character of an historian, antiquary, divine, and professor of arts and sciences, as well as a poet. In one or other of these characters he descends into many particularities which as a poet only perhaps he would have avoided. All these ought to be preserved by a faithful translator, who in some measure takes the place of Homer; and all that can be expected from him is to make them as poetical as the subject will bear. Many arts therefore are requisite to supply these disadvantages, in order to dignify and solemnize these plainer parts which hardly admit of any poetical ornaments.

Some use has been made to this end of the style of Milton. A just and moderate mixture of old words may have an effect like the working old abbey stones into a building, which I have sometimes seen to give a kind of venerable air, and yet not destroy the neatness, elegance, and equality requisite to a new work: I mean without rendering it too unfamiliar or remote from the present purity of writing, or from that ease and smoothness which ought always to accompany narration or dialogue. In reading a style judiciously antiquated, one finds a pleasure not unlike that of traveling on an old Roman way; but then the road must be as good as the way is ancient; the style must be such in which we may evenly proceed without being put to short stops by sudden abruptnesses or puzzled by frequent turnings and transpositions. No man delights in furrows and stumbling blocks; and let our love to antiquity be ever so great, a fine ruin is one thing, and a heap of rubbish another. The imitators of Milton, like most other imitators, are not copies but caricatures of their original; they are a hundred times more obsolete and cramp than he, and equally so in all places: whereas it should have been observed of Milton that he is not lavish of his exotic words and phrases everywhere alike, but employs them much more where the subject is marvelous, vast, and strange, as in the scenes of Heaven, Hell, Chaos, etc., than where it is turned to the natural and agreeable, as in the pictures of paradise, the loves of our first parents, the entertainments of angels, and the like. In general, this unusual style better serves to awaken our ideas in the descriptions and in the imaging and picturesque parts than it agrees with the lower sort of narrations, the character of which is simplicity and purity. Milton has several of the latter, where we find not an antiquated, affected, or uncouth word for some hundred lines together, as in his Fifth Book, the latter part of the Eighth, the former of the Tenth and Eleventh Books, and in the narration of Michael in the Twelfth. I wonder indeed that he who ventured (contrary to the practice of all other epic poets) to imitate Homer's lownesses in the narrative should not also have copied his plainness and perspicuity in the dramatic parts, since in his speeches (where clearness above all is necessary) there is frequently such transposition and forced construction that the very sense is not to be discovered without a second or third reading; and in this certainly he ought to be no example.

To preserve the true character of Homer's style in the present translation, great pains have been taken to be easy and natural. The chief merit I can pretend to is not to have been carried into a more plausible and figurative manner of writing, which would better have pleased all readers but the judicious ones. My errors had been fewer had each of those gentlemen who joined with me shown as much of the severity of a friend to me as I did to them in a strict animadversion and correction. What assistance I received from them was made known in general to the public in the original proposals for this work, and the particulars are specified at the conclusion of it, to which I must add (to be punctually just) some part of the Tenth and Fifteenth books.[8] The reader will now be too good a judge how much the greater part of it, and consequently of its faults, is chargeable upon me alone. But this I can with integrity affirm, that I have bestowed as much time and pains upon the whole as were consistent with the indispensable duties and cares of life and with that wretched state of health which God has been pleased to make my portion. At the least it is a pleasure to me to reflect that I have introduced into our language this other work of the greatest and most ancient of poets, with some dignity, and, I hope, with as little disadvantage as the *Iliad*. And if, after the unmerited success of that translation, anyone will wonder why I would enterprise the *Odyssey*,

8. Pope's helpers were William Broome and Elijah Fenton, but in this remark he is being less than punctually just. Pope himself translated only twelve books.

I think it a sufficient answer to say that Homer himself did the same or the world would never have seen it.[9]

9. The remainder of the *Postscript,* a continuation of Pope's quarrel with Madame Dacier, is here omitted.

CRITICISM OF DRAMA

Preface to the *Works of Shakespeare* (1725)

It is not my design to enter into a criticism upon this author, though to do it effectually and not superficially would be the best occasion that any just writer could take to form the judgment and taste of our nation. For of all English poets Shakespeare must be confessed to be the fairest and fullest subject for criticism, and to afford the most numerous as well as most conspicuous instances both of beauties and faults of all sorts. But this far exceeds the bounds of a Preface, the business of which is only to give an account of the fate of his works and the disadvantages under which they have been transmitted to us. We shall hereby extenuate many faults which are his and clear him from the imputation of many which are not: a design which, though it can be no guide to future critics to do him justice in one way, will at least be sufficient to prevent their doing him an injustice in the other.

I cannot however but mention some of his principal and characteristic excellencies, for which (notwithstanding his defects) he is justly and universally elevated above all other dramatic writers. Not that this is the proper place of praising him, but because I would not omit any occasion of doing it.

If ever any author deserved the name of an *original*, it was Shakespeare. Homer himself drew not his art so immediately from the fountains of Nature; it proceeded through Egyptian strainers and channels and came to him not without some tincture of the learning or some cast of the models of those before him. The poetry of Shakespeare was inspiration indeed; he is not so much an imitator as an instrument of Nature; and 'tis not so just to say that he speaks from her, as that she speaks through him.

His *characters* are so much Nature herself that 'tis a sort of injury to call them by so distant a name as copies of her. Those

161

of other poets have a constant resemblance, which shows that
they received them from one another and were but multipliers
of the same image: each picture, like a mock-rainbow, is but the
reflection of a reflection. But every single character in Shakespeare is as much an individual as those in life itself; it is as
impossible to find any two alike; and such as from their relation
or affinity in any respect appear most to be twins will upon comparison be found remarkably distinct. To this life and variety of
character, we must add the wonderful preservation of it, which is
such throughout his plays that, had all the speeches been printed
without the very names of the persons, I believe one might have
applied them with certainty to every speaker.

The power over our *passions* was never possessed in a more
eminent degree or displayed in so different instances. Yet all
along, there is seen no labor, no pains to raise them, no prepara-
tion to guide our guess to the effect or be perceived to lead
toward it. But the heart swells and the tears burst out just at the
proper places. We are surprised the moment we weep; and yet
upon reflection find the passion so just that we should be surprised if we had not wept, and wept at that very moment.

How astonishing is it again that the passions directly opposite
to these, laughter and spleen, are no less at his command! that he
is not more a master of the great than of the ridiculous in human
nature; of our noblest tendernesses, than of our vainest foibles;
of our strongest emotions, than of our idlest sensations!

Nor does he only excel in the passions: in the coolness of
reflection and reasoning he is full as admirable. His *sentiments*
are not only in general the most pertinent and judicious upon
every subject; but by a talent very peculiar, something between
penetration and felicity, he hits upon that particular point on
which the bent of each argument turns or the force of each motive
depends. This is perfectly amazing from a man of no education or
experience in those great and public scenes of life which are
usually the subject of his thoughts; so that he seems to have
known the world by intuition, to have looked through human
nature at one glance, and to be the only author that gives ground

for a very new opinion, that the philosopher and even the man of the world may be *born*, as well as the poet.

It must be owned that with all these great excellencies, he has almost as great defects and that as he has certainly written better, so he has perhaps written worse, than any other. But I think I can in some measure account for these defects from several causes and accidents without which it is hard to imagine that so large and so enlightened a mind could ever have been susceptible of them. That all these contingencies should unite to his disadvantage seems to me almost as singularly unlucky as that so many various (nay contrary) talents should meet in one man was happy and extraordinary.

It must be allowed that stage-poetry of all other is more particularly levelled to please the populace, and its success more immediately depending upon the common suffrage. One cannot therefore wonder if Shakespeare, having at his first appearance no other aim in his writings than to procure a subsistence, directed his endeavors solely to hit the taste and humor that then prevailed. The audience was generally composed of the meaner sort of people and therefore the images of life were to be drawn from those of their own rank; accordingly we find that not our author's only but almost all the old comedies have their scene among tradesmen and mechanics; and even their historical plays strictly follow the common old stories or vulgar traditions of that kind of people. In tragedy, nothing was so sure to surprise and cause admiration as the most strange, unexpected, and consequently most unnatural events and incidents; the most exaggerated thoughts; the most verbose and bombast expression; the most pompous rhymes, and thundering versification. In comedy, nothing was so sure to please as mean buffoonery, vile ribaldry, and unmannerly jests of fools and clowns. Yet even in these our author's wit buoys up and is borne above his subject; his genius in those low parts is like some prince of a romance in the disguise of a shepherd or peasant; a certain greatness and spirit now and then break out, which manifest his higher extraction and qualities.

It may be added that not only the common audience had no notion of the rules of writing, but few even of the better sort piqued themselves upon any great degree of knowledge or nicety that way, till Ben Jonson, getting possession of the stage, brought critical learning into vogue. And that this was not done without difficulty may appear from those frequent lessons (and indeed almost declamations) which he was forced to prefix to his first plays and put into the mouth of his actors, the *Grex, Chorus,* etc., to remove the prejudices and inform the judgment of his hearers. Till then, our authors had no thoughts of writing on the model of the Ancients; their tragedies were only histories in dialogue, and their comedies followed the thread of any novel as they found it, no less implicitly than if it had been true history.

To judge therefore of Shakespeare by Aristotle's rules is like trying a man by the laws of one country who acted under those of another. He writ to the *people,* and writ at first without patronage from the better sort and therefore without aims of pleasing them; without assistance or advice from the learned, as without the advantage of education or acquaintance among them; without that knowledge of the best models, the Ancients, to inspire him with an emulation of them; in a word, without any views of reputation and of what poets are pleased to call immortality: some or all of which have encouraged the vanity or animated the ambition of other writers.

Yet it must be observed that when his performances had merited the protection of his prince, and when the encouragement of the court had succeeded to that of the town, the works of his riper years are manifestly raised above those of his former. The dates of his plays sufficiently evidence that his productions improved in proportion to the respect he had for his auditors. And I make no doubt this observation would be found true in every instance, were but editions extant from which we might learn the exact time when every piece was composed and whether writ for the town or the court.

Another cause (and no less strong than the former) may be deduced from our author's being a *player* and forming himself first upon the judgments of that body of men whereof he was a member. They have ever had a standard to themselves, upon other principles than those of Aristotle. As they live by the majority, they know no rule but that of pleasing the present humor and complying with the wit in fashion, a consideration which brings all their judgment to a short point. Players are just such judges of what is right as tailors are of what is graceful. And in this view it will be but fair to allow that most of our author's faults are less to be ascribed to his wrong judgment as a poet than to his right judgment as a player.

By these men it was thought a praise to Shakespeare that he scarce ever "blotted a line." This they industriously propagated, as appears from what we are told by Ben Jonson in his *Discoveries* and from the preface of Heminges and Condell[1] to the first folio edition. But in reality (however it has prevailed) there never was a more groundless report, or to the contrary of which there are more undeniable evidences. As the comedy of the *Merry Wives of Windsor*, which he entirely new writ; the *History of Henry VI*, which was first published under the title of *The Contention of York and Lancaster*; and that of *Henry V*, extremely improved; that of *Hamlet* enlarged to almost as much again as at first, and many others.[2] I believe the common opinion of his want of learning proceeded from no better ground. This too might be thought a praise by some, and to this his errors have as injudiciously been ascribed by others. For 'tis certain, were it true, it could concern but a small part of them; the most are such as are not properly defects, but superfoetations, and arise not from want of learning or reading but from want of thinking or judging, or rather (to be more just to our author) from a compliance to those wants in others. As to a wrong choice of the subject, a wrong conduct of the incidents, false thoughts, forced expressions, etc., if these are not to be ascribed to the foresaid

1. Editors of the First Folio.
2. Pope's reasoning in these remarks is faulty, since he bases it on pirated copies of *Merry Wives* and *Henry V* and on the assumption that the early *Hamlet* and the *Contention of York and Lancaster* are Shakespeare's. See D. Nichol Smith, *Eighteenth Century Essays on Shakespeare* (Glasgow: J. MacLehose, 1903), p. 311.

accidental reasons, they must be charged upon the poet himself, and there is no help for it. But I think the two disadvantages which I have mentioned (to be obliged to please the lowest of people and to keep the worst of company) if the consideration be extended as far as it reasonably may, will appear sufficient to mislead and depress the greatest genius upon earth. Nay the more modesty with which such a one is endued, the more he is in danger of submitting and conforming to others, against his own better judgment.

But as to his want of learning, it may be necessary to say something more. There is certainly a vast difference between learning and languages. How far he was ignorant of the latter, I cannot determine; but 'tis plain he had much reading at least, if they will not call it learning. Nor is it any great matter, if a man has knowledge, whether he has it from one language or from another. Nothing is more evident than that he had a taste of natural philosophy, mechanics, ancient and modern history, poetical learning and mythology. We find him very knowing in the customs, rites and manners of antiquity. In *Coriolanus* and *Julius Caesar*, not only the spirit, but manners, of the Romans are exactly drawn; and still a nicer distinction is shown between the manners of the Romans in the time of the former and of the latter. His reading in the ancient historians is no less conspicuous, in many references to particular passages; and the speeches copied from Plutarch in *Coriolanus* may, I think, as well be made an instance of his learning as those copied from Cicero in *Catiline*, of Ben Jonson's. The manners of other nations in general, the Egyptians, Venetians, French, etc., are drawn with equal propriety. Whatever object of nature or branch of science he either speaks of or describes, it is always with competent, if not extensive, knowledge; his descriptions are still exact; all his metaphors appropriated and remarkably drawn from the true nature and inherent qualities of each subject. When he treats of ethic or politic, we may constantly observe a wonderful justness of distinction, as well as extent of comprehension. No one is more a master of the poetical story or has more frequent allusions to the various parts of it; Mr. Waller (who has been celebrated for this last particular) has not shown more learning this way than Shakespeare. We have translations from Ovid published in his name, among those poems which pass for his, and for some of which we have undoubted authority (being published by himself and dedicated to his noble patron, the Earl of Southampton). He appears also to have been conversant in Plautus, from whom he has taken the plot of one of his plays; he follows the Greek authors, and particularly Dares Phrygius, in another (although I will not pretend to say in what language he read them).[3] The modern Italian writers of novels he was manifestly acquainted with; and we may conclude him to be no less conversant with the Ancients of his own country from the use he has made of Chaucer in *Troilus and Cressida* and in the *Two Noble Kinsmen*, if that play be his, as there goes a tradition it was (and indeed it has little resemblance of Fletcher, and more of our author than some of those which have been received as genuine).

I am inclined to think this opinion proceeded originally from the zeal of the partisans of our author and Ben Jonson, as they endeavored to exalt the one at the expense of the other. It is ever the nature of parties to be in extremes; and nothing is so probable as that because Ben Jonson had much the most learning, it was said on the one hand that Shakespeare had none at all; and because Shakespeare had much the most wit and fancy, it was retorted on the other that Jonson wanted both. Because Shakespeare borrowed nothing, it was said that Ben Jonson borrowed everything. Because Jonson did not write extempore, he was reproached with being a year about every piece; and because Shakespeare wrote with ease and rapidity, they cried he never once made a blot. Nay the spirit of opposition ran so high that whatever those of the one side objected to the other was taken at the rebound and turned into praises, as injudiciously as their antagonists before had made them objections.

Poets are always afraid of envy; but sure they have as much reason to be afraid of admiration. They are the Scylla and Charybdis of authors; those who escape one often fall by the

3. Pope refers to the *Comedy of Errors* and *Troilus and Cressida*.

other. "The worst kind of enemies are those who praise you,"[4] says Tacitus; and Virgil desires to wear a charm against those who praise a poet without rule or reason: "Should he praise me unduly, wreathe my brow with foxglove, lest he harm the bard."[5] But however this contention might be carried on by the partisans on either side, I cannot help thinking these two great poets were good friends and lived on amicable terms and in offices of society with each other. It is an acknowledged fact that Ben Jonson was introduced upon the stage and his first works encouraged by Shakespeare. And after his death, that author writes "To the Memory of his Beloved Mr. William Shakespeare," which shows as if the friendship had continued through life. I cannot for my own part find anything invidious or sparing in those verses, but wonder Mr. Dryden was of that opinion. He exalts him not only above all his contemporaries, but above Chaucer and Spenser, whom he will not allow to be great enough to be ranked with him, and challenges the names of Sophocles, Euripides, and Aeschylus, nay all Greece and Rome at once, to equal him; and (which is very particular) expressly vindicates him from the imputation of wanting art, not enduring that all his excellencies should be attributed to Nature. It is remarkable, too, that the praise he gives him in his *Discoveries* seems to proceed from a personal kindness; he tells us that he loved the man as well as honored his memory; celebrates the honesty, openness, and frankness of his temper; and only distinguishes, as he reasonably ought, between the real merit of the author and the silly and derogatory applauses of the players. Ben Jonson might indeed be sparing in his commendations (though certainly he is not so in this instance), partly from his own nature and partly from judgment. For men of judgment think they do any man more service in praising him justly, than lavishly. I say, I would fain believe they were friends, though the violence and ill-breeding of their followers and flatterers were enough to give rise to the contrary report. I would hope that it may be with parties, both in wit and state, as with

4. *Pessimum genus inimicorum laudantes. Agricola* xli.
5. *Si ultra placitum laudarit, baccare frontem cingite, ne vati noceat. Eclogue* VII, 27–28. Translation from Fairclough.

those monsters described by the poets, and that their heads at least may have something human, though their bodies and tails are wild beasts and serpents.

As I believe that what I have mentioned gave rise to the opinion of Shakespeare's want of learning, so what has continued it down to us may have been the many blunders and illiteracies of the first publishers of his works. In these editions their ignorance shines almost in every page; nothing is more common than *Actus tertia. Exit omnes. Enter three witches solus.*[6] Their French is as bad as their Latin, both in construction and spelling; their very Welsh is false. Nothing is more likely than that those palpable blunders of Hector's quoting Aristotle,[7] with others of that gross kind, sprung from the same root, it not being at all credible that these could be the errors of any man who had the least tincture of a school or the least conversation with such as had. Ben Jonson (whom they will not think partial to him) allows him at least to have had *some* Latin, which is utterly inconsistent with mistakes like these. Nay the constant blunders in proper names of persons and places are such as must have proceeded from a man who had not so much as read any history, in any language, so could not be Shakespeare's.

I shall now lay before the reader some of those almost innumerable errors, which have risen from one source, the ignorance of the players, both as his actors and as his editors. When the nature and kinds of these are enumerated and considered, I dare to say that not Shakespeare only, but Aristotle or Cicero, had their works undergone the same fate, might have appeared to want sense as well as learning.

It is not certain that any one of his plays was published by himself. During the time of his employment in the theater, several of his pieces were printed separately in quarto. What makes me think that most of these were not published by him is the excessive carelessness of the press; every page is so scandalously false

6. This blunder seems to have been invented by Pope. See Smith, *Eighteenth Century Essays on Shakespeare*, p. 313.

7. The anachronism occurs in *Troilus and Cressida*, Act II, scene 2, l. 166.

spelled, and almost all the learned or unusual words so intolerably mangled, that it's plain there either was no corrector to the press at all or one totally illiterate. If any were supervised by himself, I should fancy the two parts of *Henry IV* and *Midsummer Night's Dream* might have been so, because I find no other printed with any exactness; and (contrary to the rest) there is very little variation in all the subsequent editions of them. There are extant two prefaces, to the first quarto edition of *Troilus and Cressida* in 1609 and to that of *Othello,* by which it appears that the first was published without his knowledge or consent and even before it was acted, so late as seven or eight years before he died, and that the latter was not printed till after his death. The whole number of genuine plays which we have been able to find printed in his lifetime amounts but to eleven. And of some of these, we meet with two or more editions by different printers, each of which has whole heaps of trash different from the other, which I should fancy was occasioned by their being taken from different copies, belonging to different playhouses.

The folio edition (in which all the plays we now receive as his, were first collected) was published by two players, Heminges and Condell, in 1623, seven years after his decease. They declare that all the other editions were stolen and surreptitious, and affirm theirs to be purged from the errors of the former. This is true as to the literal errors and no other; for in all respects else it is far worse than the quartos.

First, because the additions of trifling and bombast passages are in this edition far more numerous. For whatever had been added, since those quartos, by the actors, or had stolen from their mouths into the written parts, were from thence conveyed into the printed text, and all stand charged upon the author. He himself complained of this usage in *Hamlet,* where he wishes that "those who play the Clowns would speak no more than is set down for them." (Act iii. Sc. iv.) But as a proof that he could not escape it, in the old editions of *Romeo and Juliet* there is no hint of a great number of the mean conceits and ribaldries now to be found there. In others, the low scenes of mobs, plebeians and clowns are vastly shorter than at present. And I have seen one in

particular (which seems to have belonged to the playhouse, by
having the parts divided with lines and the actors' names in the
margin) where several of those very passages were added in a
written hand, which are since to be found in the folio.

In the next place, a number of beautiful passages which are
extant in the first single editions are omitted in this, as it seems
without any other reason than their willingness to shorten some
scenes: these men (as it was said of Procrustes) either lopping, or
stretching an author, to make him just fit for their stage.

This edition is said to be printed from the original copies; I
believe they meant those which had lain ever since the author's
days in the playhouse and had from time to time been cut, or
added to, arbitrarily. It appears that this edition, as well as the
quartos, was printed (at least partly) from no better copies than
the prompter's book, or piecemeal parts written out for the use
of the actors; for in some places their very names are through
carelessness set down instead of the *personae dramatis*.[8] And in
others the notes of direction to the property-men for their mov-
ables, and to the players for their entries, are inserted into the
text, through the ignorance of the transcribers.[9]

The plays not having been before so much as distinguished
by acts and scenes, they are in this edition divided according as
they played them; often where there is no pause in the action, or
where they thought fit to make a breach in it, for the sake of
music, masques, or monsters.

Sometimes the scenes are transposed and shuffled backward
and forward, a thing which could no otherwise happen, but by
their being taken from separate and piecemeal-written parts.

Many verses are omitted entirely, and others transposed, from
whence invincible obscurities have arisen, past the guess of any

8. *Much Ado about Nothing*, Act II. "Enter Prince Leonato, Claudio, and
Jack Wilson," instead of "Balthasar." And in Act IV, "Cowley and Kemp,"
constantly through a whole scene. Edit. Fol. of 1623 and 1632 [Pope].
9. Such as,
"My Queen is murdered! *Ring the little bell.*"
"His nose grew as sharp as a pen, *and a table of Greenfield's,*" etc.
[Pope]

commentator to clear up, but just where the accidental glimpse of an old edition enlightens us.

Some characters were confounded and mixed, or two put into one, for want of a competent number of actors. Thus in the quarto edition of *Midsummer Night's Dream*, Act V, Shakespeare introduces a kind of Master of the Revels called Philostratus, all whose part is given to another character (that of Aegeus) in the subsequent editions. So also in *Hamlet* and *King Lear*. This too makes it probable that the prompter's books were what they called the original copies.

From liberties of this kind, many speeches also were put into the mouths of wrong persons, where the author now seems chargeable with making them speak out of character; or sometimes perhaps for no better reason that that a governing player, to have the mouthing of some favorite speech himself, would snatch it from the unworthy lips of an underling.

Prose from verse they did not know, and they accordingly printed one for the other throughout the volume.

Having been forced to say so much of the players, I think I ought in justice to remark that the judgment, as well as condition, of that class of people was then far inferior to what it is in our days. As then the best playhouses were inns and taverns (the Globe, the Hope, the Red Bull, the Fortune, etc.), so the top of the profession were then mere players, not gentlemen of the stage. They were led into the buttery by the steward, not placed at the lord's table or lady's toilette, and consequently were entirely deprived of those advantages they now enjoy in the familiar conversation of our nobility and an intimacy (not to say dearness) with people of the first condition.

From what has been said, there can be no question but had Shakespeare published his works himself (especially in his latter time, and after his retreat from the stage) we should not only be certain which are genuine but should find in those that are the errors lessened by some thousands. If I may judge from all the distinguishing marks of his style and his manner of thinking and writing, I make no doubt to declare that those wretched plays, *Pericles, Locrine, Sir John Oldcastle, Yorkshire Tragedy, Lord*

Cromwell, The Puritan, and *London Prodigal,* cannot be admitted as his. And I should conjecture of some of the others (particularly *Love's Labor's Lost, The Winter's Tale,* and *Titus Andronicus*) that only some characters, single scenes, or perhaps a few particular passages were of his hand. It is very probable what occasioned some plays to be supposed Shakespeare's was only this: that they were pieces produced by unknown authors or fitted up for the theater while it was under his administration; and no owner claiming them, they were adjudged to him, as they give strays to the lord of the manor: a mistake which (one may also observe) it was not for the interest of the house to remove. Yet the players themselves, Heminges and Condell, afterwards did Shakespeare the justice to reject those eight plays in their edition, though they were then printed in his name, in everybody's hands, and acted with some applause (as we learn from what Ben Jonson says of *Pericles* in his Ode on the *New Inn*). That *Titus Andronicus* is one of this class I am the rather induced to believe by finding the same author openly express his contempt of it in the Induction to *Bartholomew Fair,* in the year 1614, when Shakespeare was yet living. And there is no better authority for these latter sort than for the former, which were equally published in his lifetime.

If we give into this opinion, how many low and vicious parts and passages might no longer reflect upon this great genius, but appear unworthily charged upon him? And even in those which are really his, how many faults may have been unjustly laid to his account from arbitrary additions, expunctions, transpositions of scenes and lines, confusion of characters and persons, wrong application of speeches, corruptions of innumerable passages by the ignorance, and wrong corrections of them again by the impertinence, of his first editors? From one or other of these considerations, I am verily persuaded that the greatest and grossest part of what are thought his errors would vanish and leave his character in a light very different from that disadvantageous one in which it now appears to us.

This is the state in which Shakespeare's writings lie at present; for, since the above-mentioned folio edition, all the rest have implicitly followed it, without having recourse to any of the former or ever making the comparison between them. It is impossible to repair the injuries already done him; too much time has elapsed, and the materials are too few. In what I have done I have rather given a proof of my willingness and desire, than of my ability, to do him justice. I have discharged the dull duty of an editor, to my best judgment, with more labor than I expect thanks, with a religious abhorrence of all innovation, and without any indulgence to my private sense or conjecture. The method taken in this edition will show itself. The various readings are fairly put in the margin so that every one may compare them; and those I have preferred into the text are constantly *ex fide codicum*, upon authority. The alterations or additions which Shakespeare himself made are taken notice of as they occur. Some suspected passages which are excessively bad (and which seem interpolations by being so inserted that one can entirely omit them without any chasm, or deficience in the context) are degraded to the bottom of the page, with an asterisk referring to the places of their insertion. The scenes are marked so distinctly that every removal of place is specified, which is more necessary in this author than any other, since he shifts them more frequently; and sometimes without attending to this particular, the reader would have met with obscurities. The more obsolete or unusual words are explained. Some of the most shining passages are distinguished by commas in the margin; and where the beauty lay not in particulars but in the whole, a star is prefixed to the scene. This seems to me a shorter and less ostentatious method of performing the better half of criticism (namely the pointing out an author's excellencies) than to fill a whole paper with citations of fine passages, with general applauses or empty exclamations at the tail of them. There is also subjoined a catalogue of those first editions by which the greater part of the various readings and of the corrected passages are authorized (most of which are such as carry their own evidence along with them). These editions now hold the place of originals and are the only materials left to repair the deficiencies or restore the corrupted sense of the author. I can only wish that a greater number of them (if a greater were ever published) may yet be found, by a search more successful than mine, for the better accomplishment of this end.

I will conclude by saying of Shakespeare, that with all his faults and with all the irregularity of his drama, one may look upon his works, in comparison of those that are more finished and regular, as upon an ancient majestic piece of Gothic architecture, compared with a neat modern building. The latter is more elegant and glaring, but the former is more strong and more solemn. It must be allowed that in one of these there are materials enough to make many of the other. It has much the greater variety and much the nobler apartments, though we are often conducted to them by dark, odd, and uncouth passages. Nor does the whole fail to strike us with greater reverence, though many of the parts are childish, ill-placed, and unequal to its grandeur.

INDEX

Addison, Joseph, x, 128; and the Ancients, xii; and the rules, xxi; quoted, 73, 74

Aeschylus, 168

Allegory, 37

Ancients, the, to be imitated, 6, 7–8, 13, 26; and Moderns, 43–45; modernizing of, 76

Anticlimax, 69

Apollonius, 110

Arbuthnot, John, xvi, xvii, 40–42

Aristotle, xv, xx, xxiv, 6, 10, 44, 81, 112, 114, 169; his criticism praised, 19; on invention, 109; compares *Iliad* and *Odyssey*, 150; his rules and Shakespeare, 164

Asgill, John, 76

Atterbury, Francis, xii, xxvii

Augustus, 41

Avellaneda, Alonso Fernandez de la, 10

Behn, Aphra, 75

Belianis of Greece, 85

Bible, the, and Homer's style, 123

Bion, 104

Blackmore, Sir Richard, xix, 14, 53, 61; quoted and criticized, 50–78 *passim*

Boileau (Despréaux), Nicholas, xxi, 21, 41, 119; *Le Lutrin*, 153

Bolingbroke, Henry St. John, First Viscount, 37–39, 129

Bonarelli, Guidobaldo, 34

Booth, Barton, 87

Bouhours, Dominique, xxi

Broome, William, 54, 57, 157

Brown, Thomas, 76

Burnet, Thomas, 86

Carnarvon, James Brydges, Earl of, 129

Cato, 69

Cervantes Saavedra, Miguel de, *Don Quixote*, 39; style of, 153

Chapman, George, 126

Chaucer, Geoffrey, xvi, 167, 168

Cibber, Colley, 54, 70, 78, 87

Cicero, Marcus Tullius, 33, 40, 76, 154, 166, 169

Cleveland, John, 59

Codrington, Christopher, 54

Coleridge, S. T., xxiii

Condell, Henry, 165, 170, 173

Congreve, William, xxi, 128

Crane, R. S., xii–xiii, xxiii

Crashaw, Richard, his poetry criticized, 35–37

Critics, Pope's opinion of, ix, 3–22 *passim*, 23, 131–132

Cromwell, Henry, 30–33, 35–37

Curll, Edmund, 55

Dacier, Anne Lefèvre, xxvi, 118, 149, 158

Dares Phrygius, 167

Defoe, Daniel, 54, 61

Demosthenes, 33, 40, 154

Denham, Sir John, 12; *Cooper's Hill*, 136

Dennis, John, ix, x, xxi, 10, 54; attacks *Essay on Criticism*, xxiv, 18 n.; quoted, 69, 78; his project for the stage, 87

Dionysius of Halicarnassus, 20, 33, 116

Domitian, 42

Donne, John, 29

Dryden, John, xxi, 19, 168; on Shakespeare, xv; defines drama, xxiii; sound and sense in, xxx, 32–33; attacks upon him, 14; his language to become obsolete, 15; on wit, 30;

177